KING'S DAUGHTER,
LET'S CELEBRATE!
believe your regal identity.
DISCOVER A-Z REGAL LIVING
SECRETS
FROM THE KING'S HEART TO YOURS.
experience
radiant joy.
LIVE YOUR LIFE
WITH KINGDOM PURPOSE.
learn truth.
TRADE UP
TO ABUNDANT LIFE IN JESUS.
live regally in reality
—*one secret at a time!*

THANKS a MILLION!

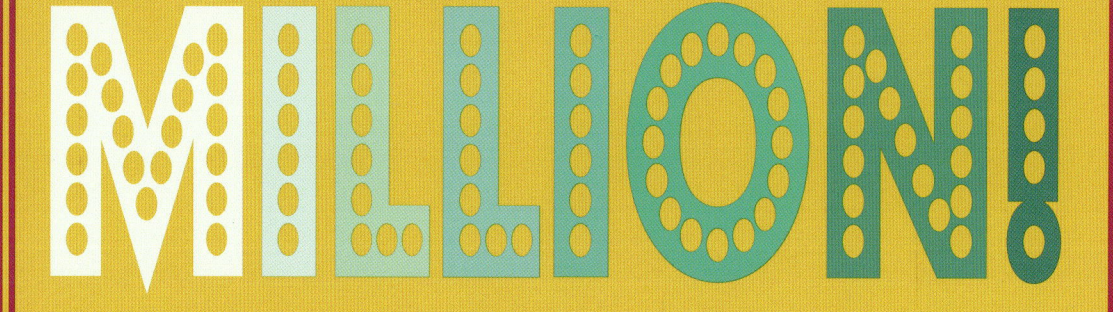

"The secret of the Lord is with them that fear Him." Psalm 25:14

FIRST WE WOULD LIKE TO SAY
THANK YOU

TO THE FATHER

We give glory and honor to the Lord God Almighty
and King of the Universe! Thank you, Father. You are *"merciful and
gracious, long-suffering, and abounding in goodness and truth" (Ex. 34:6).*

TO THE SON

Thank you, Jesus, for sacrificing Your life so that we could
live in an intimate relationship with God and
receive *"life and life more abundantly" (John 10:10).*

TO THE HOLY SPIRIT

Thank you, Holy Spirit, for revealing God's Word and
making each Regal Living Secret personal to us and to our readers.
*"The Spirit searches all things, even the deep things of God. Now we have
received...the Spirit who is from God, that we might know the things that
have been freely given to us by God" (1 Cor. 2:10,12).*

TO OUR ENCOURAGERS

Thank you to our pastors, family, friends, editors, and prayer warriors.
Your godly wisdom, fervent prayers, and steadfast encouragement
bless us more than you can imagine! *"I thank my God every time I
remember you...I always pray with joy because of your
partnership in the gospel" (Phil. 1:3-5).*

KING'S DAUGHTERS™

LET'S CELEBRATE WOMEN AND GIRLS WITH TRUTH AND BEAUTY!

TRADING UP BOOK SERIES • SPEAKING • FINE ART • GIFTS

ABOUT THE AUTHORS:

In 1988, the Lord called Ginnie Johansen Johnson to trade in her worldly identity as a fashion designer and trade up to her regal identity in Christ. "Praise God for His relentless pursuit to transform a stressed out **high achiever** into one of the **happiest receivers** in Christ," says Ginnie. *Trading Up for a King's Daughter* is Ginnie's "thank you note" to the King for giving her each Regal Living Secret—freely, creatively, and abundantly. It is now Ginnie's honor to share *Trading Up* with you! Ginnie is a wife, mother of three daughters, fine artist, and prolific writer. Her Scripture packed, creative speaking engagements, 'Regal Celebrations,' ignite women as King's daughters inside and out. Find Ginnie's story on page 90.

During Sarah Johnson's senior year at the University of Texas, the Lord spoke to her: "Go back to Dallas and I will send you all over the world." She obeyed His voice and became the co-writer and graphic designer of *Trading Up for a King's Daughter*. She writes and sings songs to complement many chapters of this book (find song titles in chapter page corners and listen online). The Lord has Sarah a heart for middle school, high school, and college age girls to understand their identity in Christ. Sarah speaks and sings to groups all over the country, sharing her testimony, music, and *Trading Up for a King's Daughter*. Find Sarah's story on page 92.

HOW TO USE *TRADING UP*

Trading Up Small Group
Use with Study Guide. See page 97.

The Perfect Gift!
Keep stocked for any occasion.

Trading Up Regal Celebration
Hospitality for Christ! See page 96.

Personal Devotional
Answer core chapter questions in your journal. See page 15.

Trading Up Live Event
Invite Ginnie & Sarah to speak in your city. See page 94.

Mother-Daughter Study
Go through each Regal Living Secret together.

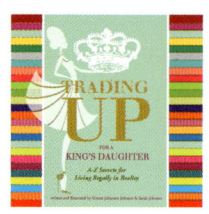

TABLE OF CONTENTS

TRADING UP IS BECAUSE OF JESUS..................................11
TRADING UP INTRODUCTION..13
REGAL IDENTITY AS A KING'S DAUGHTER......................18
REGAL RELATIONSHIP WITH THE KING............................20
REGAL LIVING SECRETS • A-Z..23

    Secret #1: **A**ccepting God's Perfect Love..................25
    Secret #2: **B**eginning Your Day with Abba Father.......27
    Secret #3: **C**elebrating at the Father's Party.............29
    Secret #4: **D**eclaring Christ in You............................31
    Secret #5: **E**xpressing Christ through You..................33
    Secret #6: **F**inding Security in Christ........................35
    Secret #7: **G**oing to God's Word..............................39
    Secret #8: **H**earing God's Voice................................41
    Secret #9: **I**nterceding in Prayer For & With Others.....43
    Secret #10: **J**oyfully Receiving Abundant Life.............45
    Secret #11: **K**nowing God's Names............................47
    Secret #12: **L**iving in the Holy Spirit's Power..............51
    Secret #13: **M**oving Over for God's Perfect Orchestration.....55
    Secret #14: **N**on-Stop Loving in Christ......................57

Secret #15: **O**beying God's Word & Voice..................................59
Secret #16: **P**raying the Lord's Prayer.......................................61
Secret #17: **Q**uenching the enemy's Darts................................63
Secret #18: **R**ejoicing in Trials by Faith....................................65
Secret #19: **S**peaking God's Promises.....................................67
Secret #20: **T**hanking Jesus for His Finished Work of the Cross........69
Secret #21: **U**nderstanding the Mystery of Israel.....................71
Secret #22: **V**aluing Godly Womanhood.................................75
Secret #23: **W**orshipping God...77
Secret #24: "**X**-pressing" His Workmanship.............................79
Secret #25: **Y**ielding to Divine Appointments.........................81
Secret #26: **Z**ealously Doing Greater Works...........................83

Prayer of Salvation..86
King's Daughters Causes..87

APPENDIX

Ginnie's *Trading Up* Story..90
Sarah's *Trading Up* Story..92
Sarah's Music for *Trading Up*..93
Need a Speaker?..94
Your *Trading Up* Regal Celebration......................................96
Trading Up for Small Group Bible Studies............................97
King's Daughters Art & Gift Collection....................................99

Trading Up for a King's Daughter • A-Z Secrets for Living Regally in Reality
Written, Illustrated, and Designed by Ginnie Johansen Johnson and Sarah Johnson
Copyright © 2013 by King's Daughters
ISBN 978-0-9960926-0-9

All rights reserved. No part of this publication may be reproduced, stored in a retrieval system, or transmitted in any form or by any means—electronic, mechanical, photocopy, recording, or any other—except for brief quotations in printed reviews, without the prior permission of the publisher. All Scripture is from The New King James Version unless otherwise noted. Scripture taken from the New King James Version. Copyright © 1982 by Thomas Nelson, Inc. Used by permission. All rights reserved. Scripture quotations noted NIV are from The Bible, New International Version. New York: Biblica: 2011. Scripture quotations noted KJV are from THE KING JAMES VERSION - Strong's Concordance, Nashville TN, T. Nelson Publishers 1996. Though we are not ordained pastors, this book has been edited by ordained pastors. This is a discipleship oriented tool and an expression of our gratitude to God our Father for His abundant Regal Living Secrets. Any thoughts you have are valued and welcomed.

TRADING UP
IS ALL BECAUSE OF JESUS

*"For **by grace** you have been saved **through faith**,
and that not of yourselves; it is the gift of God,
not of works, lest anyone should boast." Ephesians 2:8-9*

"The Heart Spangled Banner"
The Gospel to the tune of *The Star Spangled Banner*

O say can you see
By His blood shed for me?
Sin and death will not reign,
For His victory remains.

By His stripes we are healed,
Through His sacrificed life.
He died on Calvary—
Dead to sin and so are we.

We cry Abba Father.
We're the children of God.
Joint-heirs with our Lord—
By His Spirit we're one.

Oh How I will declare
That His love has set me free!
Oh sweet glorious liberty
The secret of Christ in me.

Melody by John Stafford Smith, 1780 • Lyrics ©Ginnie Johnson with Anna Terry
Inspired by Romans 8

TRADE IN | TRADE UP

*"Giving thanks to the Father who has qualified us to be partakers of the inheritance of the saints in the light. He has delivered us from the **power of darkness** and transferred us into the **kingdom of His dear Son.**"*
Colossians 1:12-13

TRADE IN	TRADE UP
FEAR	PERFECT LOVE
INSECURITY	SECURITY
CONFUSION	PURPOSE
STRESS	PEACE
EXHAUSTION	POWER
DEPRESSION	FULLNESS OF JOY
ANXIETY	REST
DEFEAT	VICTORY

TRADING UP INTRODUCTION

Dear King's Daughter,

The moment that you believe in Jesus Christ as your Savior,* you are rescued from darkness and given a regal identity as a King's Daughter in God's family.

*"Giving thanks to the Father who has...delivered us from the **power of darkness** and transferred us into the **kingdom of His dear Son**"* (Col. 1:12-13 - illustrated on left page).

So why are King's Daughters still living in the darkness from which they have been delivered: fearful, insecure, confused, stressed, exhausted, depressed, anxious, and defeated? Why is *royalty* still living in rags—given treasure, but tolerating trash?

Trading Up for a King's Daughter is a Scripture packed, creative tool to help you receive the kingdom upgrade that Jesus' life, death, and resurrection made possible for you. Receive perfect love, security, peace, power, fullness of joy, rest, and victory in Christ.

Today is the day to **TRADE IN** and **TRADE UP**!

TRADE IN the ways of the world, sin of the flesh, and lies of the devil.
TRADE UP to God's ways, God's will, and God's abundant life for you in Christ.

Trading Up for a King's Daughter is not about trying harder to be a "good Christian." It is not about "working on yourself." It is all about receiving the love of the Father, the life of the Son, and the power of the Holy Spirit.

There are two parts of this book. In Part I, we explain your regal **identity** as a King's Daughter and describe an intimate **relationship** with the Lord. In Part II, we express 26 **Regal Living Secrets** from God's Word. We pray these secrets equip you to live in God's divine order and divine blessing.

Are you ready to "live regally in reality"—living with unshakable identity, radiant joy, and kingdom purpose? The King wants you to **TRADE UP** and receive His fullness *"on earth as it is in heaven" (Matt. 6:10).* Let's Celebrate!

— *Ginnie Johnson & Sarah Johnson*

*Prayer of Salvation on Page 86

VIDEO:
Trading Up Intro

TRADING UP INTRODUCTION

TRADING UP
TERMS TO KNOW

KING'S DAUGHTER
A BELIEVER IN JESUS CHRIST WHO IS
A MEMBER OF GOD'S ROYAL FAMILY
AND A CO-HEIR WITH CHRIST.

LIVING REGALLY IN REALITY
LIVING WITH UNSHAKABLE IDENTITY,
RADIANT JOY, AND KINGDOM PURPOSE IN CHRIST.

REGAL LIVING SECRETS
LIFESTYLE SECRETS FOUND IN GOD'S WORD
FOR LIVING IN HIS DIVINE ORDER
AND DIVINE BLESSING.

TRADE IN:
REFUSING THE WAYS OF THE WORLD,
SIN OF THE FLESH, AND LIES OF THE DEVIL.
RETURNING TO GOD BY REPENTANCE AND FAITH.

TRADE UP:
SEEKING GOD'S FACE TO KNOW HIS WILL.
FOLLOWING HIS WORD IN CHRIST'S POWER.
RECEIVING THE ABUNDANT LIFE THAT FOLLOWS.

TRADING UP IS AN INTERACTIVE BOOK!
QUESTIONS + SONG OR VIDEO PER CHAPTER

ASK *TRADING UP'S*
CHAPTER QUESTIONS

These core questions apply to every chapter of *Trading Up*! Discuss them in your small group or answer them in a personal journal.

1.) What did you discover about God, Jesus, or the Holy Spirit?

2.) What is your favorite verse in this chapter and why?

3.) **TRADE IN**: What do you want to trade in? Refuse the world, the flesh, and the devil. Return to God by repentance and faith.

4.) **TRADE UP**: How will you apply this Regal Living Secret in your every day life? How will this bless you?

5.) What did you receive from this chapter's song, "interactive," or artistic illustration?

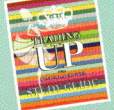
Trading Up Study Guide on page 97

WATCH *TRADING UP'S*
INTRO VIDEO

Meet the authors and hear God's heart for you as a King's daughter. Also find more chapter videos with personal stories and more!

LISTEN TO *TRADING UP'S*
ORIGINAL MUSIC

Co-author Sarah Johnson writes and sings powerful original songs for many chapters.

FIND MUSIC & VIDEOS
ONLINE

As you read *Trading Up,* find each chapter's song or video online.
www.kings-daughters.com

VIDEO & SONG TITLES IN THE CORNER TABS

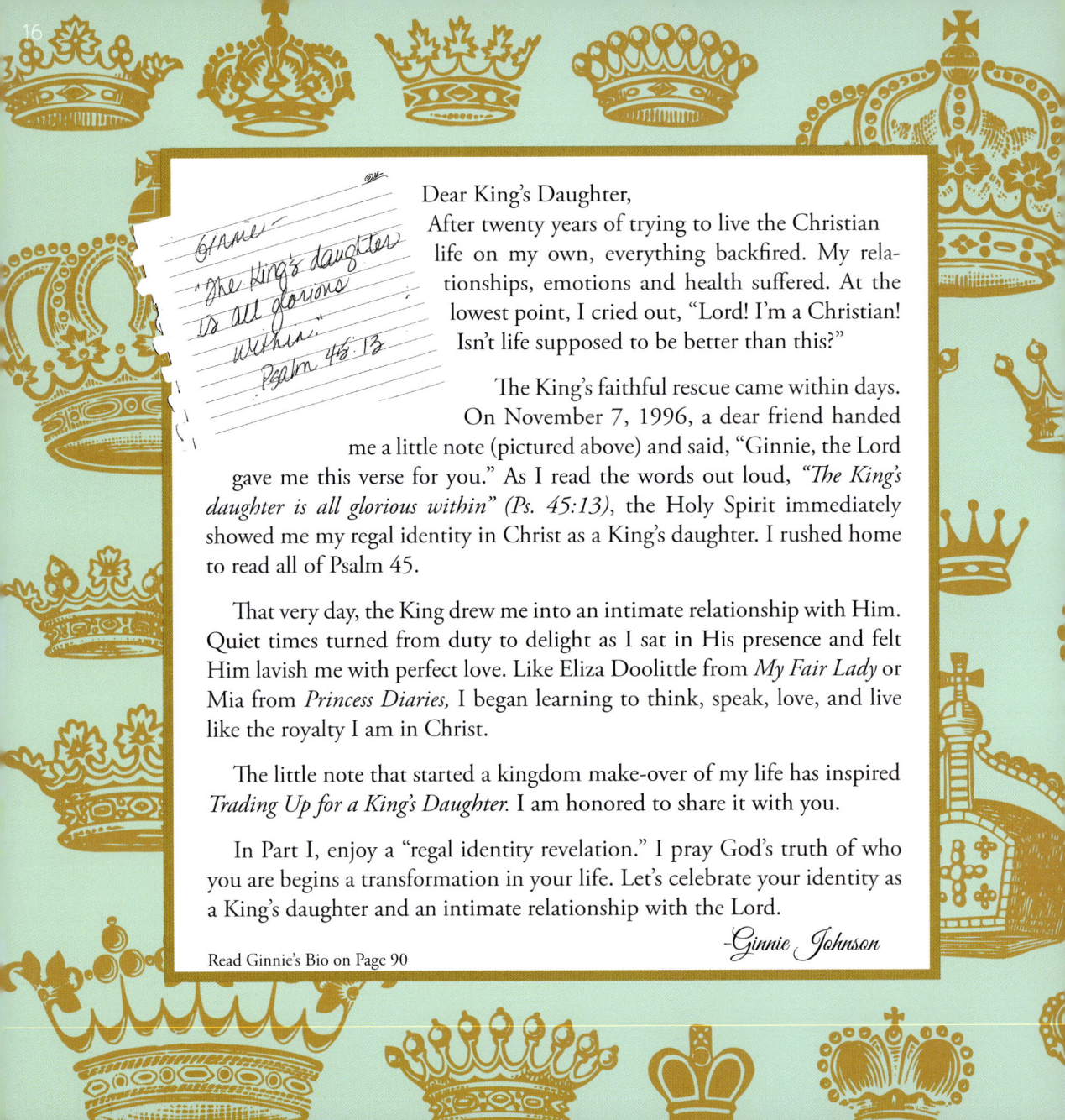

Dear King's Daughter,

After twenty years of trying to live the Christian life on my own, everything backfired. My relationships, emotions and health suffered. At the lowest point, I cried out, "Lord! I'm a Christian! Isn't life supposed to be better than this?"

The King's faithful rescue came within days. On November 7, 1996, a dear friend handed me a little note (pictured above) and said, "Ginnie, the Lord gave me this verse for you." As I read the words out loud, *"The King's daughter is all glorious within" (Ps. 45:13)*, the Holy Spirit immediately showed me my regal identity in Christ as a King's daughter. I rushed home to read all of Psalm 45.

That very day, the King drew me into an intimate relationship with Him. Quiet times turned from duty to delight as I sat in His presence and felt Him lavish me with perfect love. Like Eliza Doolittle from *My Fair Lady* or Mia from *Princess Diaries,* I began learning to think, speak, love, and live like the royalty I am in Christ.

The little note that started a kingdom make-over of my life has inspired *Trading Up for a King's Daughter.* I am honored to share it with you.

In Part I, enjoy a "regal identity revelation." I pray God's truth of who you are begins a transformation in your life. Let's celebrate your identity as a King's daughter and an intimate relationship with the Lord.

-Ginnie Johnson

Read Ginnie's Bio on Page 90

PART I

TRADING UP

YOUR REGAL IDENTITY AS A KING'S DAUGHTER

A REGAL RELATIONSHIP WITH THE KING

YOUR REGAL IDENTITY AS A KING'S DAUGHTER

Dear King's Daughter,

If you have put your faith in Jesus Christ as your Savior and Lord*, you are a King's daughter! You have been adopted by God and given a whole new identity in Christ. The idea of being a King's daughter comes from God's Word. Ask the Holy Spirit to illuminate each word of Psalm 45:13 below.

"THE KING'S daughter is all glorious WITHIN" Psalm 45:13.

THE KING'S • Note the possessive apostrophe on King**'s**. You belong to the King of kings! He says to you, *"Fear not, I have called you by your name. You are Mine," (Isaiah 43:1).* He will never leave nor forsake you. The King is ALL powerful for you, ALL knowing of you, and ALL loving towards you.

daughter • You are a cherished member of God's royal family, given access to the fullness of His love and provision. You are not a slave nor a hired hand for God. You are a daughter—an **heir** of God. *"Now if we are children, then we are heirs—heirs of God and co-heirs with Christ" (Rom. 8:16-17).* As a King's daughter, everything Jesus has is yours. Everything Jesus is, you are. *"As He is, so are we in this world" (1 John 4:17).*

is • It does not say "The King's daughter will be"—nor "when she is good enough"—nor "in heaven" —nor "trying to be." In Christ, the King's daughter **IS** all glorious within. Your regal identity is sealed at salvation. It is final!

all glorious WITHIN • You are filled with the glorious life of Christ to live regally in reality. *"To them God willed to make known what are the riches of the glory of this mystery...which is Christ in you, the hope of glory" (Col. 1:27).* **When you know Who you have within, you won't go without.**

*Prayer of Salvation on Page 86

The King of Kings

regally invites you!

"Listen, O daughter,

....

(write your full name)

Consider and incline your ear;

Forget your own people also, and your father's house;

So the King will greatly desire your beauty;

Because He is your Lord, worship Him."

Psalm 45:9-11

A REGAL RELATIONSHIP WITH THE KING

What a glorious identity you have as a King's Daughter! But it doesn't stop there. Psalm 45 also reveals the **regal relationship** the King desires to have with you. Receive His invitation to you on the left page by signing your name on the royal dotted line.

> "**Listen**, O Daughter, **consider**, and **incline** your ear;
> **Forget** also your own people, and **forget** your father's house.
> So the King will greatly desire your beauty.
> Because He is your Lord, **worship** Him...
> The King's daughter is all glorious within...
> With gladness and rejoicing they shall be brought;
> They shall enter the King's palace." Psalm 45:10-15

The King, your loving Heavenly Father, greatly desires to be close to you. He is your Maker and the Lover of your soul. He is perpetually loving, guiding, planning, preparing, sanctifying, and increasing your life in Him. You were created for an intimate relationship Him.

God beckons you to listen, consider, and incline your ear to hear His voice. Forget all pressure from the world and receive His presence. Forget all guilt from past mistakes and receive His grace. Forget all performance and be loved. He delights in spending time with you. He greatly desires your **beauty**. Because He is your Lord, worship Him. Notice a King's Daughters' trademark is gladness and rejoicing—an overflow of her connection with the King.

Co-author Sarah Johnson wrote this song about a regal relationship with the King. Let the lyrics be a prayer to the King!

Now that you know your **regal identity in Christ as a King's daughter** and what it means to live in a **regal relationship with the King**, let's discover **A-Z Regal Living Secrets** from God's Word.

Made for You
©Sarah Johnson 2013

I was made for You—
every part of me.
I was made for You.
Every broken piece
gets put back together
when You hold me tight.
When You talk to me,
all the world seems right.
So pull me closer.
Draw me nearer.

All I want is all of You.
All You want is all of me.
So I'll sit with you a while
till Your face is all I see.

I was made to hear
every word You say.
It's like the world disappears
when You say my name.
It's the sweetest sound
that I'll ever know.
The only thing I've found
that makes me whole.
So tell me more.
Tell me everything.

All I want is all of You.
All You want is all of me.
So I'll sit with You a while
till Your face is all I see.

You're all I want
and all I need
All I want
and all I need!

SARAH'S SONG:
Made for You

REGAL LIVING SECRETS • A–Z

	TRADE IN	TRADE UP
Secret #1: **A**ccepting God's Perfect Love	FEAR	PERFECT LOVE
Secret #2: **B**eginning Your Day with Abba	PERFORMANCE	RELATIONSHIP
Secret #3: **C**elebrating at the Father's Party	REBELLION OR PRIDE	HUMILITY
Secret #4: **D**eclaring Christ in You	OLD MAN	NEW CREATION
Secret #5: **E**xpressing Christ through You	SELF-EFFORT	FAITH
Secret #6: **F**inding Security in Christ	INSECURITY & SORROW	SECURITY & RADIANCE
Secret #7: **G**oing to God's Word	FOOLISHNESS	WISDOM
Secret #8: **H**earing God's Voice	MY WILL	GOD'S WILL
Secret #9: **I**nterceding For & With Others	INTERFERENCE	INTERCESSION
Secret #10: **J**oyfully Receiving Abundant Life	HELL ON EARTH	HEAVEN ON EARTH
Secret #11: **K**nowing God's Names	LACK	TOTAL PROVISION
Secret #12: **L**iving in the Holy Spirit's Power	POWERLESSNESS	POWER
Secret #13: **M**oving Over for God's Orchestration	CONTROL	TRUST
Secret #14: **N**on-Stop Loving in Christ	BITTERNESS	UNCONDITIONAL LOVE
Secret #15: **O**beying God's Word & Voice	CONSEQUENCES	BLESSINGS
Secret #16: **P**raying the Lord's Prayer	PARTIAL COVERAGE	FULL COVERAGE
Secret #17: **Q**uenching the enemy's Darts	VICTIM MIND-SET	VICTOR MIND-SET
Secret #18: **R**ejoicing in Trials by Faith	HOPELESSNESS	HOPE & FAITH
Secret #19: **S**peaking God's Promises	NEGATIVE WORDS	GOD'S PROMISES
Secret #20: **T**hanking Jesus for His Finished Work of the Cross	ISSUES & ILLNESS	HEALING
Secret #21: **U**nderstanding the Mystery of Israel	IGNORANCE	GOD'S HEART FOR ISRAEL
Secret #22: **V**aluing Godly Womanhood	VANITY	VIRTUE
Secret #23: **W**orshipping God	DEPRESSION & WORRY	FULLNESS OF JOY
Secret #24: **"X**-pressing" God's Workmanship	MY WORKS	HIS WORKS
Secret #25: **Y**ielding to Divine Appointments	DISAPPOINTMENTS	DIVINE APPOINTMENTS
Secret #26: **Z**ealously Doing Greater Works	BUSYNESS	GREATER WORKS

PART II

TRADING UP

FOR A
KING'S DAUGHTER

A - Z
REGAL LIVING SECRETS

REGAL LIVING SECRET #1

ACCEPTING GOD'S PERFECT LOVE

"God is love, and he who abides in love abides in God, and God in Him... There is no fear in love; but perfect love casts out fear, because fear involves torment.... We love Him because He first loved us." 1 John 4:16, 18,19

Dear King's Daughter,

Accepting God's love is the beginning of living regally in reality. *"I pray...that you being rooted and grounded in God's love, may be able to comprehend what is the width, length, depth, and height of His love" (Eph. 3:14-18).* God's perfect love is wide enough to cover your every need, deep enough to heal your every sorrow, and high enough to fulfill your every hope. It is unconditional, limitless, and unchanging. He loves you when you make a mistake. He loves you when others decide they don't. God IS love. *"I have loved you with an everlasting love: therefore with loving-kindness I have drawn you" (Jer. 31:3).* When you truly accept God's perfect love, fear flees. His *"perfect love casts out all fear" (1 John 4:18).* Fear of God's love changing based on your good or bad behavior: gone! Fear of rejection from people: a thing of the past! "One day I had a vertical encounter with God's love that truly ended my horizontal pursuit of looking to others for love," says Ginnie, "God gave me a vision where I was plucking a daisy saying, 'He loves me, I love me.'" Go buy a daisy plant and TRADE UP to God's kingdom "daisy affirmation." Pluck each petal repeating the words, "He loves me, I love me, He loves me, I love me." Beloved, be loved!

TRADE IN:	TRADE UP:
FEAR	PERFECT LOVE
doubting God's perfect love	accepting God's perfect love

SARAH'S SONG: Let Me Love You

Where is your chair?

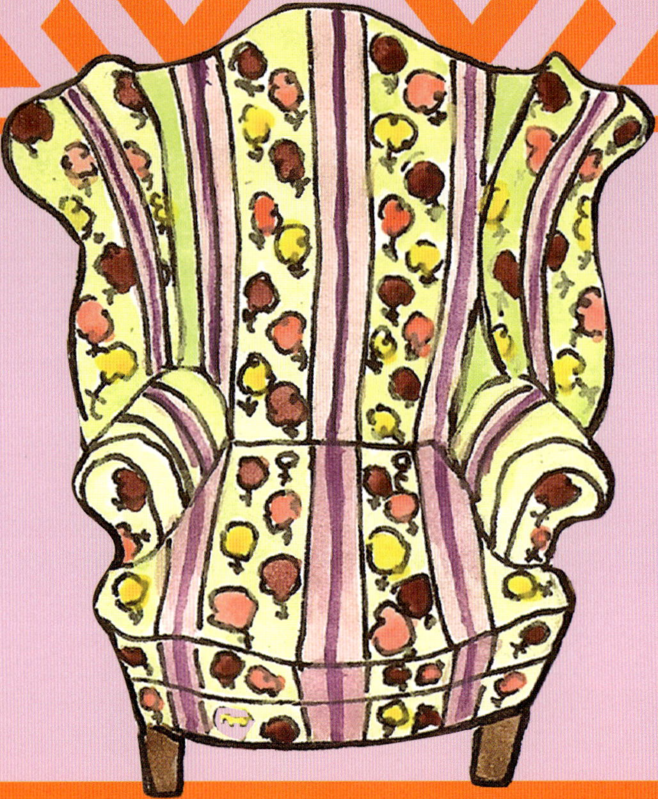

"Just come sit in my lap. Don't fix up. You can't do it on your own anyway. I didn't want you to serve Me, work for Me, or to be a great blessing for Me. I just wanted to be with you. Let's just waste time together. Let's take extravagant, unhurried time together." - your Abba Father

(as told by Pastor Jim Borchert)

REGAL LIVING SECRET #2

Beginning Your Day with Abba Father

"Come to Me all who are weary and burdened, and I will give you rest." Matthew 11:28

Dear King's Daughter,

Abba means "Daddy" in Hebrew—what an intimate term to call God your Father! *"Because you are sons, God has sent forth the Spirit of His Son into your hearts, crying out, "Abba, Father!" Therefore you are no longer a slave but a son, and if a son, then an heir of God through Christ" (Gal. 4:6-7).* What freedom to begin your day with Abba each morning—sitting on His lap and feeling His arms hold you close to His heart. This was your Abba Father's plan when He created you: a Daddy-daughter relationship. The second you wake up, He eagerly awaits to spend time with you. Yes, you! Even though there are seven billion people on this earth, God desires one-on-one time with you—**just as you are.** Imagine the sorrow in the Father's heart when He sees His children slaving away to be "good Christians" instead of spending time with Him. Good behavior does not create intimacy with God. Breathe a deep sigh of relief. The exhaustion of performance ends today. *"Come to Me all who are weary and burdened, and I will give you rest"* (Matt. 11:28). Where is a comfy chair where you can begin your day with Abba and experience His delight in you? Sit at His feet before you get on your feet. Be captivated!

TRADE IN: PERFORMANCE	TRADE UP: RELATIONSHIP
doing for God—trying to be a "good Christian"	beginning your day with Abba—just as you are

SARAH'S SONG: I'm Amazed

Crowns of Destiny
Ginnie Johnson
Acrylic on Canvas

=== REGAL LIVING SECRET #3 ===

CELEBRATING
WITH THE FATHER

"Let us celebrate! ALL that I have is yours." Luke 15:23,31

Dear King's Daughter,

Every day, your Heavenly Father invites you to celebrate with Him and receive His ALL. Jesus' blood rolled out the royal red carpet that gives you access to the Father's party. Take a moment to read the story of the prodigal son in Luke 15. Notice three "GALS" in the story: the prodiGAL running from the father (Luke 15:12-17), the leGAL working for the father (Luke 15:25-32), and the reGAL celebrating with the father (Luke 15:18-24). Get a picture of the King's full throttle party. There is music, laughter, and dancing! King's daughter, wherever you are, whatever you have done, your Heavenly Father invites you to come home. Come just as you are—and as fast as you can. Just say with humility, "Father, I'm tired of doing life my own way. I want to come home!" Can you see your Heavenly Father running to greet you? He throws His arms around you and kisses you. He removes your rags of shame and clothes you with His robe of righteousness, His ring of authority, and His slippers of rest. His eyes, sparkling with anticipation, look into yours. He says, "*Let us celebrate! **ALL** that I have is yours*" (Luke 15:23,31). The King is a celebratory Father. You are His celebrated heir. TRADE UP and go celebrate like one! All that He has is yours!

TRADE IN:
REBELLION OR PRIDE
running from or working for the Father

TRADE UP:
HUMILITY
celebrating with the Father

SARAH'S SONG:
Come Home

OLD MAN MINDSET

NEW CREATION MINDSET

*"If anyone is in Christ, he is a new creation; **old things** have passed away, behold, **all things** have become **new**"*
2 Corinthians 5:17

LIVING IN THE SINS OF THE FLESH:
Sexual immorality
Impurity
Sensuality
Idolatry
Witchcraft
Hatred
Discord
Jealousy
Fits of Rage
Selfish Ambition
Dissensions
Factions
Envy
Drunkenness
Orgies
and the like
GALATIANS 5:19-21

SIN NATURE

NIV • Sensuality from NASB

DECLARING CHRIST IN YOU:
"LOVE
JOY
PEACE
PATIENCE
GOODNESS
GENTLENESS
FAITH
MEEKNESS
AND SELF-CONTROL"
GALATIANS 5:22

REGAL LIVING SECRET #4

DECLARING
CHRIST IN YOU

"To them God willed to make known what are the riches of the glory of this mystery among the Gentiles: which is Christ in you, the hope of glory." Colossians 1:27

Dear King's Daughter,

At your salvation, God replaced your old sin nature with a new divine nature. You are a new creation, filled with the very life of Jesus Christ. *"If anyone is in Christ, he is a new creation; old things have passed away, behold, all things have become new" (2 Cor. 5:17).* Your old sin nature was crucified and buried with Christ (Rom. 6). That old man is dead—over and out. God does not look at you and see a sinner, a liar, a perfectionist, a gossip, a failure, a high achiever, an addict, nor a stress case. God looks at you and sees the righteousness of His Son, Jesus (2 Cor. 5:21). *"To them God willed to make known what are the riches of the glory of this mystery among the Gentiles: which is Christ in you, the hope of glory" (Col. 1:27).* As you understand this mystery of Christ within, you will break out of strongholds of sin, guilt, shame, and condemnation. *"There is now no condemnation to those who are in Christ Jesus, who do not walk according to the flesh, but according to the Spirit" (Rom. 8:1).* Declaring Christ in you is the first step to expressing His character and power in every day life. *"We have this treasure in earthen vessels, that the excellence of the power may be of God and not of us" (2 Cor. 4:7).* Ask the Holy Spirit to change your mindset so you walk, talk, love, and live like the new creation you are!

TRADE IN:	TRADE UP:
OLD MAN MINDSET	NEW CREATION MINDSET
seeing yourself as the old man living in sin & shame of the flesh	seeing yourself as a new creation & declaring Christ in you

To go deeper in this truth, read Romans 6-8.

VIDEO:
The Amethyst
Illustration

"I have been crucified with Christ nevertheless I live yet not I but Christ liveth in me and the life which I now live in the flesh I live by the faith of the Son of God who loved me and gave Himself for me."

Galatians 2:20

"The Lord gave me this watercolor during a quiet time studying Galatians 2:20. Notice the powerful, bold words in the cross beams. I also encourage you to artistically illustrate verses that are significant to you. -Ginnie

REGAL LIVING SECRET #5

EXPRESSING CHRIST THROUGH YOU

*"I have been crucified with Christ: nevertheless I live; yet not I, but Christ lives in me: and the life which I now live in the flesh **I live by the faith of the Son of God**, who loved me, and gave Himself for me." Galatians 2:20*

Dear King's Daughter,

   Now that you have declared Christ IN you, are you ready to express Christ THROUGH you? Receiving this secret starts with humbly saying, *"Apart from Him I can do nothing" (John 15:5)*—but *"I can do all things **through Christ** who strengthens me" (Phil. 4:13).* Daily declare your flesh crucified with Christ and receive a fresh reminder that the very life and faith of Jesus Christ is in you to do all things. It takes faith to believe that Jesus will equip you *"both to will and to do God's good pleasure" (Phil. 2:13).* Praise God that He gave you the very faith of His Son Jesus! Not a single ounce of self effort is needed. In fact, it only gets in the way of Christ living through you. Go ahead and remove the phrases, "I'm working on...." or "I'm trying to...." or "I am striving to" out of your vocabulary. Christ's life ignites you as a godly woman, friend, student, wife, mother, volunteer, sister, professional, and daughter! To let Christ express Himself through you, die daily to the flesh and *declare Christ's life in you* (tip: lie on the floor and say Galatians 2:20). Arise for a faith-filled day *expressing Christ through you.*

TRADE IN:
SELF-EFFORT
living in flesh apart from Christ

TRADE UP:
CHRIST THROUGH YOU
daily dying to the flesh and expressing Christ through you

♪ SARAH'S SONG: All Things

Royal Thoughts
Ginnie Johnson
Acrylic on Canvas

REGAL LIVING SECRET #6

Finding Security in Christ

"How precious to me are Your thoughts, O God! How vast is the sum of them! Were I to count them, they would outnumber the grains of sand." Psalm 139:17-18

Dear King's Daughter,

    Don't you love the beach imagery in Psalm 139? God's thoughts for you are more than the sands of the sea! Your Creator delights in every detail about you, from your personality and body type to the way you smile and worship. You are His marvelous masterpiece, fearfully and wonderfully made in His image (Psalm 139:14). *"He is enthralled with your beauty" (Psalm 45:11).* With the beach as our backdrop, let's get on the King's wave length. Let Him turn the tide of your mind-set to see yourself as He sees you. The days of searching for security in people, places, and things are over! Who wants to waste another day living by feelings—going up and down with what others think or don't think of you? When you find your security in God's thoughts, you live with a radiance no person or circumstance can dull. *"Those who look to Him are radiant!" (Ps. 34:5).* On the next page, look into the "Kingdom Mirror" the Lord gave Ginnie—complete with a two minute song to memorize God's incredible thoughts towards you. His thoughts are worth counting. Your insecurities are worth leaving behind.

TRADE IN:
INSECURITY & SORROW
searching for security in
people, places, and things

TRADE UP:
SECURITY & RADIANCE
finding security
in Christ alone

GINNIE'S SONG:
I am Accepted

Approval, Activities, Appearance, Awards
Beauty, Background, Boyfriends, Business, Body
Clothing, Children, Clubs, College, Compliments
Degrees, Diet, Designer labels, Donations
Economic status, Education, Engagement rings
Family, Furnishings, Finances, Failures, Friends
Goals, Gifts, Grades, Giving, Gadgets
Houses, Home life, Health, Husband
Intelligence, Image, Invitations, Income level
Job, Jewels
Knowledge, Kids' accomplishments
Leisure, Looks, Leadership positions
Money, Motherhood, Material things, Marriage
Neighborhood, Name recognition
Occupational status, Opportunities
Positions, Possessions, Popularity, Performance, Pay Checks
Quality and Quantity of belongings
Respect, Reputation, Rank, Results, Recognition
Skills, Salary, Success, Self, Schools, Social Media
Travel, Titles, Talents, Thank You Notes
Upward class mobility
Vitality, Vacations
Wealth, Weight, Wins, Work, Wife role
Xtra-ordinary accomplishments
Youth, Your connections
Zip Code, Zodiac signs

INSECURITY

This worldly mirror exposes people, places, and things that we can often look to for security. ***"The sorrows of those will increase who run after other gods" (Ps. 16:4).*** Trade In the insecurity and sorrow that comes from looking to false gods in this mirror.

I am **A**ccepted Eph. 1:6
I am **B**eloved Eph. 1:6
I am **C**omplete in Him Col. 2:10
totally **D**elivered Col. 1:13
Established in Him Heb. 13:9
Forgiven for all my sins 1 John 1:9
I am **G**rounded Eph. 3:7
Heir to the King 1 Peter 3:7
Indwelled with the Spirit Himself Rom. 8:11
Joint-Heir with Jesus Rom. 8:17
Kept in His Love Jude 1:21
Loved with an everlasting love Jer. 31:3
totally **M**ade Alive in Christ 1 Cor. 15:22
a **N**ew Creation, I am 2 Cor. 5:17
an **O**vercomer 1 John. 5:4
Peculiar, too Titus 2:14
Quieted from all my fears Ps. 34:4
I am **R**edeemed, Repaired, Restored John 3:16
Set free, Sanctified 1 Thes. 5:23
Taught of the Lord Isa. 54:13
Understood by my King Heb. 4:15
a **V**ictor in everything I Cor. 15:57
I am His **W**orkmanship Eph. 2:10
Xtra Special Ps. 139
Yielded Rom. 6:13
Zealously built-up Col. 2:7

SECURITY

This Kingdom Mirror expresses just 29 of God's infinite thoughts for you! The mirror can be sung to "16 Going on 17" from *The Sound of Music*. It's a two minute song and an instant identity boost.
"Those who look to Him are radiant!" (Ps. 34:5)
Melody by Rodgers and Hammerstein

ABIDING John 15:1-8	**HELP FROM GOD** Isaiah 43:1-4	**MONEY** 1 Timothy 6:10	**STRENGTH** Psalm 73:26
BLESSING Deuteronomy 28:1-14	**HEALING** Isaiah 53:1-4	**NEEDS** Philemon 4:19	**SCHOOL** Proverbs 21:5
BURDENS Matthew 11:30	**INTIMACY WITH GOD** Isaiah 43:1-4	**OBEDIENCE** Isaiah 1:21	**TEMPTATION** 2 Peter 2:9
COMFORT 2 Corinthians 1:3-4	**JOY IN TRIALS** James 1:2-4	**PRAYER** Matthew 6:6-9	**TRUTH** John 8:26
CHILDREN Psalms 127	**JUDGEMENT** 2 Chronicles 1:10	**PROSPERITY** Psalm 122:6	**UNDERSTANDING** Ephesians 1:7-8
CONFIDENCE Hebrews 4:16	**KINDNESS** Ephesians 4:29-32	**POWER** Romans 8:8	**UNITY** Psalm 133:1
DRINKING Ephesians 5:18	**LOVING GOD** Luke 10:27	**PROTECTION** Psalm 91	**VICTORY** 1 Corinthians 15:57-58
DIRECTION Psalm 143:8	**LOVING YOURSELF** Luke 10:28	**PERSECUTION** 2 Corinthians 12:10	**WISDOM** James 1:5
DEPRESSION Psalm 42:5-11	**LOVING OTHERS** Matthew 5:44-48	**PERSEVERANCE** Galatians 6:9	**WEALTH** Deuteronomy 8:18
FUTURE Jeremiah 29:11	**LONG LIFE** Psalm 91:16	**PATIENCE** Romans 15:4-5	**WOMANHOOD** Proverbs 31:10-31
GIVING 2 Corinthians 9:8,11	**MARRIAGE** Ephesians 5:21-33	**RESPECT** James 2:1	**WORRIES** Philemon 4:19
FORGIVENESS Mark 11:25-26	**MOTHERHOOD** Titus 2:1-5	**REST** Matthew 11:27-29	**ZEAL** Romans 12:1
HONORING PARENTS Ephesians 6:2			

REGAL LIVING SECRET #7

GOING TO GOD'S WORD

"As for God, His way is perfect: The Lord's Word is flawless" 2 Samuel 22:31

Dear King's Daughter,

What if at any given moment, you could call God and ask His flawless advice on any matter big or small—and receive an immediate, clear answer? The Bible makes this possible. Every verse opens a window into the very wisdom and heart of God. *"All Scripture is given by inspiration of God, and is profitable for doctrine, for reproof, for correction, for instruction in righteousness, that the man of God may be complete, thoroughly equipped for every good work" (2 Tim. 3:16-17).* Whatever your question, problem, or need, let Scripture's flawless wisdom guide you to God's perfect will. We are constantly bombarded with advice, trends, and ideas from the world. God calls the wisdom of the world foolishness (1 Cor. 3:19). It only leads to downfall. Jesus asks, *"Are you not mistaken because you do not know the Scriptures or the power of God?" (Mark 12:24).* Let God's Word be a lamp unto your feet and a light unto your path (Psalm 119:105). Find Scriptures for your current needs in your Bible concordance or from our list of 50 verses on the left page. BONUS: Discover 176 fascinating benefits of God's Word in Psalm 119. Here are just three benefits to start the list: answers, great peace, and extraordinary insight.

TRADE IN: FOOLISHNESS
going to the world's advice FIRST

TRADE UP: WISDOM
going to God's Word FIRST

SARAH'S SONG: Promises

Trees of Righteousness
Ginnie Johnson
Acrylic on Canvas

REGAL LIVING SECRET #8

HEARING GOD'S VOICE

Listen to your "GodPod" every day!

"He who is of God hears God's words." John 8:47

Dear King's Daughter,

Hearing God's voice is one of the highest privileges for a King's daughter. "*He who is of God hears God's words*" (John 8:47). Let's look at the blessings of hearing and submitting to God's voice.

- **Love:** "*Cause me to hear Your loving kindness in the morning*" (Ps. 143:8).
- **Peace:** "*He will speak peace to His people*" (Ps. 85:8).
- **Guidance:** "*Your ears will hear a voice behind you, saying, 'This is the way; walk in it'*" (Isa. 30:21).
- **Holiness:** God says, "*Obey My voice, and I will be your God, and you shall be My people. And walk in all the ways that I have commanded you, that it may be well with you*" (Jer. 7:23).
- **Freedom from pride:** "*He guides the humble in what is right and teaches them His way*" (Ps. 25:9).
- **Wisdom:** "*I will...show you great and mighty things, which you do not know*" (Jer. 33:2-3).

Ultimately, God's voice forms you into a holy vessel, set apart to display God's love and glory to the world. Don't let over-thinking, selfishness, nor distractions cause you to make independent decisions that can detour you from your destiny. Jesus lived "*by every word that proceeds from the mouth of God*" (Matt. 4:4)—and so can you! Declare by faith, "God, I thank You that I live by every word that proceeds from Your mouth!" Listen for the unique, specific ways He will speak to you.

TRADE IN:	TRADE UP:
MY WILL	GOD'S WILL
steering your life	hearing God's voice

SARAH'S SONG: *All of Me*

FAMILY MEMBERS
SPOUSE
CHILDREN
FRIENDS
COWORKERS
THE POOR
CHURCHES
GRANDCHILDREN

"I DO NOT CEASE TO PRAY FOR YOU."
COLOSSIANS 1:9

MISSIONARIES
NEIGHBORS
THE SICK
POLITICAL LEADERS
WIDOWS & ORPHANS
ENEMIES
THE LOST
WHO ELSE?

REGAL LIVING SECRET #9

INTERCEDING
IN PRAYER FOR & WITH OTHERS

"I do not cease to pray for you..." Colossians 1:9

Dear King's Daughter

Did you know that Jesus is sitting at the right hand of God interceding for you right now? *"He ever lives to make intercession for [you]" (Heb. 7:25).* Let us follow Jesus' example and intercede for others. Ask the Lord to bring to mind someone in your life who needs prayer and put their name in Paul's powerful prayer of intercession. *"For this reason we also, since the day we heard it, do not cease to pray for _____, and to ask that _____ may be filled with the knowledge of His will in all wisdom and spiritual understanding; that _____ may walk worthy of the Lord, fully pleasing Him, being fruitful in every good work and increasing in the knowledge of God; strengthened with all might, according to His glorious power, for all patience and long-suffering with joy" (Col 1:9-11).* For more kingdom "impact," join in agreement with another believer. Jesus says, *"If two of you agree on earth concerning anything that they ask, it will be done for them by My Father in heaven" (Matt. 18:18-19).* Who needs you to intercede on their behalf? If you have the opportunity, ask them Jesus' question, *"What would you have the Lord do for you?"* (Matt. 20:32)—and pray accordingly. Ask the Holy Spirit for a relevant Scripture specifically for them.

TRADE IN:
INTERFERENCE
interfering to fix someone's problem—without prayer

TRADE UP:
INTERCESSION
interceding in prayer for and with others

▶ VIDEO: Interceding for you

"THE THIEF COMES TO STEAL, KILL & DESTROY, **BUT I** HAVE COME THAT YOU MIGHT HAVE LIFE AND HAVE IT MORE **ABUNDANTLY**"!

- JESUS IN JOHN 10:10

ABUNDANTLY IN GREEK MEANS:

SUPERIOR IN QUALITY

SUPERIOR IN QUANTITY

HAVING ENOUGH TO SPARE
EXCEEDING NEED
OVER AND ABOVE; OVERFLOWING
MORE THAN IS NECESSARY;
EXCEEDING ABUNDANTLY
SUPREMELY MORE
EXTRAORDINARY
SURPASSING
UNCOMMON
REMARKABLE.
MORE EXCELLENT
STRONG'S CONCORDANCE G4053 - PERISSOS

Ginnie's oldest daughter, Elizabeth.

REGAL LIVING SECRET #10

JOYFULLY RECEIVING
ABUNDANT LIFE IN CHRIST

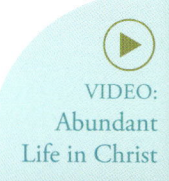

Jesus said, "The thief does not come except to steal, and to kill, and to destroy: I have come that you might have life and have it more abundantly." John 10:10

Dear King's Daughter,

Did you know Jesus came to give you a life with superior relationships, remarkable opportunities, and unsurpassed provision? Read the elaborate Greek meaning of the word "abundant" line by line on the left page. This is the kingdom standard for abundant life in Christ. Jesus paid the price to bring heaven to earth—and heaven personally into your life. From sunrise to sunset, God is going before you, beside you, and behind you arranging everything for your blessing and His glory *"on earth as it is in heaven" (Matt. 6:10).* Don't let the devil carry out his plan to steal your worship, kill your joy, and destroy your family, health, finances, and more. If a thief broke in and robbed your house, you wouldn't just stand by and say, "Oh, and take the jewelry too!" It's time for King's daughters to have zero-tolerance for the devil's agenda to bring hell on earth. Remember, the devil has been defeated. Though his attacks will come, stand firm in your inheritance of abundant life in Christ. How do you receive it? *"But seek first the kingdom of God and His righteousness, and all these things shall be added to you" (Matt. 6:33).*

TRADE IN:	TRADE UP:
HELL ON EARTH	HEAVEN ON EARTH
allowing satan to steal, kill, and destroy	joyfully receiving abundant life in Christ

VIDEO: Abundant Life in Christ

Names of God Wheel

Inner ring (names): Yeshua · Xactly Who I Need · God of Zion · Abba · Beloved · Comforter · Door · Emmanuel · Father · God of Abraham, Isaac, & Jacob · Healer · I Am · Jealous · King · Light · Maker · Name Above All Names · Omega · Provider · Quieter Of My Soul · Restorer · Savior · Truth · Understanding High Priest · Victor · Warrior

Middle ring (attributes): Worship · Strength · Hope · Liberty · Belonging · Comfort · Access · Presence · Approval · Blessings · Health · Destiny · Purity · Authority · Direction · Worth · Humility · Urgency · Provision · Security · Wholeness · Freedom · Wisdom · Grace · Triumph · Victory

Outer ring (scripture references): Psalm 103:1-5 · Phil 4:13 · Ps. 146:5,10 · Rom 8:21 · Song 2:16 · John 14:26 · John 10:9 · Matt 1:23 · 1 John 14:8 · Gen. 12:2-3 · Isa 53:5 · Ex 3:14-15 · Ex. 34:14 · 2 Tim. 1:7 · Psalm 119:105 · Psalm 139 · Phil 2:9 · Rev. 1:11 · Gen. 22:14 · Isa 30:15 · Joel 2:25-27 · Rom 6 · Psalm 119 · Heb. 4:16 · 2 Cor. 2:14 · 2 Chr. 20

REGAL LIVING SECRET #11

KNOWING GOD'S NAMES

"Bless the Lord, O my soul; and all that is within me, bless His holy Name! Bless the Lord, O my soul, and forget not all His benefits." Psalm 103:1-2

Dear King's Daughter,

If you want to know God in a deeper way, get to know His Names. The Lord has over 100 Names that reveal specific attributes of His character and benefits of His divine provision for you. He is the mighty Warrior who gives you victory, the Maker who gives you worth, and the Savior who gives you freedom. Whatever your trial or need, there is a Name of God to call upon and receive breakthrough. *"The Name of the Lord is a strong tower; The righteous run to it and are safe" (Prov. 18:10).* "One day, the Lord described Himself to me in the most vivid way," says Sarah, "He said, 'I am like a kaleidoscope. My nature never changes. But every time you look at Me, you see different sides of who I am.'" Take a moment to look at the A-Z list of God's Names on the kaleidoscope to the left. Discover different sides of who God is and how He wants to provide for you personally. Let us fall more deeply in love with our King as we know and bless His holy, wonderful Name. *"Let those also who love Your Name be joyful in You" (Psalm 5:11).* Celebrate God's Names with the declaration on the next two pages.

TRADE IN:
LACK
not knowing God's Names
—forgetting His benefits

TRADE UP:
BENEFITS
knowing God's Names
—receiving His benefits

♪ SARAH'S SONG: Love To Sing Your Name

NAMES OF GOD • A-Z

Fear, you will no longer grip me—for my
Abba gives me **liberty** (Rom. 8:21).

Rejection, you will no longer discount me—for my
Beloved gives me **belonging** (Song. 2:16).

Despair, you will not take over—for my
Comforter gives me **peace** (John 12:16).

Intimidation, you will not isolate me—for the
Door gives me **access** to the throne of God (John 10:9).

Loneliness, you will not haunt me—for
Emmanuel surrounds me with His **presence** (Psalm 16:11).

Performance, you will not drive me—for my
Father gives me **approval** unconditionally (1 John 14:8).

Family strife, you will not cause division—for the
God of Abraham, Isaac, & Jacob gives us **unity** (Gen. 12:2-3).

Disease, you will not destroy me—for my
Healer gives me health and **healing** (Isa. 53:4-5).

Condemnation, you will not disqualify me—for the great
I AM leads me into my **kingdom destiny** (Ex. 3:14-15).

Idols, you will not steal my worship—for my God's Name is
Jealous who draws me to **purity** (Ex. 34:14).

Fear, you will not torment me—for my
King gives me **authority** over the enemy (2 Tim. 1:17).

Confusion, you will not detour me—for the
Light shows me specific **directions** (Psalm 119:105).

Unworthiness, you will not shame me—for my
Maker gives me **worth and value** (Psalm 139).

Pride, you will not pollute my heart—for the **Name Above All Names** gives me humility (Phil. 2:9).

Busyness, you will not keep me from divine appointments—for the **Omega** sends me with kingdom urgency (Rev. 1:11).

Worry, you cannot cancel my faith—for my **Provider** gives me perfect provision (Gen. 22:14).

Stress, you will not rattle me—for the **Quieter Of My Soul** gives me strength and rest (Isa. 30:15).

Disappointment, you will not discourage me—for my **Restorer** gives me renewed opportunities (Joel 2:25-27).

Sin, you will not derail me from my path—for at the cross my **Savior** gave me freedom from sin (Rom. 6).

Deception, you will not mislead me—for the **Truth** gives me wisdom and clarity (Psalm 119).

Guilt, you cannot plague me—for my **Understanding High Priest** gives me mercy and grace (1 John 1:9).

Victim mentality, you will not persist—for my **Victor** causes me to triumph in Christ (2 Cor. 2:14).

Defeat, you will not have dominion—for my **Warrior** fights for me and gives me victory (2 Chron. 20).

Complaining, you will not proceed from my mouth—for my God is **X-actly Who I Need** gives me a heart of worship (Psalm 103:1-5).

Helplessness, you will not paralyze me—for **Yeshua** gives me strength to do all things in Christ (Phil. 4:13).

Uncertain future, you will not cause panic—for the **God of Zion** gives me hope (Psalm 146:5,10).

THE HOLY SPIRIT

abides in you. John 14:16

dwells in you. John 14:17

guides you. John 16:13

sanctifies you. Romans 15:16

glorifies Jesus. John 16:14

fills you with righteousness, peace, and joy. Romans 14:17

intercedes for you. Romans 8:26

reminds you. John 14:26

searches the deep things of God. 1 Corinthians 2:9-10

convicts and cleanses you. Romans 8:13

leads you. Romans 8:14

quickens you. 1 Peter 3:18

teaches you. John 14:26

reveals plans God has prepared. 1 Corinthians 2:10

bears the fruit of the Spirit. Galatians 5:22-23

lives with you forever. John 14:15

renews your mind. Titus 3:5, Romans 12:2

pours God's love into your hearts. Romans 5:5

fellowships with you. Philippians 2:1

anoints you with the seven fold anointing. Isaiah 11:1-2

REGAL LIVING SECRET #12

Living in the Holy Spirit's Power

"The Father will give you another Helper, that He may abide with you forever." John 14:16

Dear King's Daughter,

Do you ever feel like you could use a little more help in life? Jesus anticipated your need and gave you the solution: the Helper, the Holy Spirit. Jesus said, *"I will pray to the Father, and He will give you another Helper (the Holy Spirit), that He may abide with you forever" (John 14:16)*. Study the Holy Spirit's powerful role in your life on the left page. You were created to live in *"righteousness, peace, and joy in the Holy Spirit" (Rom. 14:17)*. Do not grieve the Holy Spirit by neglecting or limiting His power. When you let the Holy Spirit do His perfect work in you, His fruit follows. You exude *love*, burst with *joy*, feel *peace* during stressful times, show *patience* and *kindness* to all, speak with *gentleness*, exhibit *goodness* and *faithfulness*, and practice *self-control* (Gal. 5:22-23). Every morning, stay in God's presence until you receive a fresh outpouring of the Holy Spirit's power. Ask for the seven-fold anointing of the Holy Spirit: *"The Spirit of the Lord (which is **love**) will rest on him— the Spirit of **wisdom** and of **understanding**, the Spirit of **counsel** and of **might**, the Spirit of the **knowledge** and **fear of the LORD**" (Isaiah 11:1-2)*. But wait! There is even more! Discover 19 spiritual gifts of the Holy Spirit on the next page.

TRADE IN: POWERLESSNESS	TRADE UP: POWER
neglecting or limiting the Holy Spirit's power	living in the Holy Spirit's power

SARAH'S SONG:
Living Water

SPIRITUAL GIFTS

Spiritual Gift Teaching
© Dr. Robert Mawire
used with permission

Prophecy
- Speaking directly from God
- Understanding mysteries
- Revelation

Rom 12:6
1 Cor. 12:29-32
1 Cor. 13:2

Teaching
- Communicates the truth
- Simplification of Ideas
- Imparts understanding

Rom 12:7 · 1 Cor. 12:28
Eph. 4:11
Acts 18:26

Pastor
- Shepherding a flock of God
- Love and teaching

Eph. 4:11
Rom. 12:7
Acts 20:28-31

Workers of Miracles
- People fear God
- Signs and wonders

1 Cor. 12:10
Acts 5:9-11

Discernment
- The ability to understand spiritual activity
- Expose false teachers and satanic activity

1 John 4:1
1 Cor. 12:10

Healing
- Divine cures
- Complete restoration
- Healing from sickness & disease

Acts 3:6-7
1 Cor. 12:9

Words of Knowledge
- Revelation about people
- The truth about the situation

1 Cor. 12:8
1 Cor. 2:6-12

Wisdom
- Divine wisdom
- Revelation insights

1 Cor. 12:8

Mercy
- Showing loving kindness to others
- Compassion

1 Cor. 14:27-28
Rom. 12:8

Interpretation of tongues
- Translation of tongues
- Interpreting someone's personal prayer language to God.

1 Cor. 12:10
1 Cor. 14:27-28

Tongues
- Speaking a personal prayer language to God.

1 Cor. 12:10
Romans 8:26-27

Faith
- The grace to expect miracles
- Accomplishing great things by faith

1 Cor. 12:9

Encouragement
- Comforting & strengthening
- Instructing in love
- Encouragement of the Body of Christ

Rom 12:8

Helping Service
- Giving practical assistance Meeting felt needs

Rom 12:7

Administration
- Organization
- Order/Structure

Titus 1:5
Rom 12:8

Evangelism
- Presenting the gospel with clarity
- Winning souls

Eph. 4:11

Giving
- Giving liberally & cheerfully
- Meeting physical needs

Acts 9:36
Rom 12:8

Apostleship
- Planting churches/ Rulership
- Establishing Order
- Embodying each gift

1 Cor. 12:28
Eph. 4:11, Gal. 1

Hospitality
- Welcoming & entertaining guests, often in your home, with great joy and kindness.

Rom. 12:13

20+ VERBS
Verses on page 50

19 GIFTS
Romans 12:1
1 Corinthians 12:1-26

YOU CAN COUNT ON THE HOLY SPIRIT!

9 FRUITS
Galatians 5:22-23

7 FOLD ANOINTING
Isaiah 11:1

THE HOLY SPIRIT'S VERBS, FRUIT, ANOINTING, AND GIFTS IGNITE YOUR LOVE FOR THE KING AND EQUIP YOU TO LOVE OTHERS!

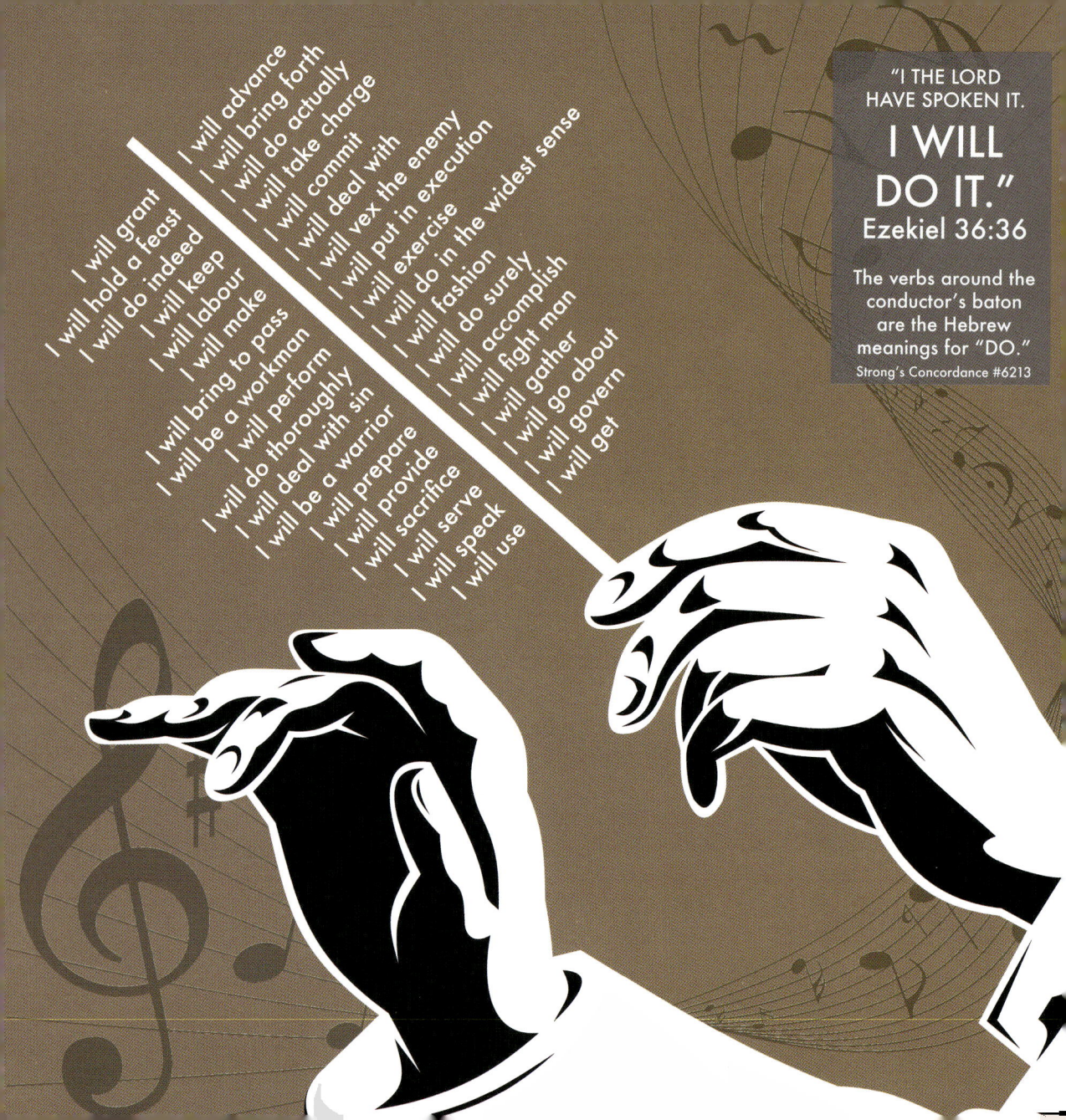

"I THE LORD HAVE SPOKEN IT.

I WILL DO IT."
Ezekiel 36:36

The verbs around the conductor's baton are the Hebrew meanings for "DO."
Strong's Concordance #6213

- I will grant
- I will hold a feast
- I will do indeed
- I will keep
- I will labour
- I will make
- I will bring to pass
- I will be a workman
- I will perform
- I will do thoroughly
- I will deal with sin
- I will be a warrior
- I will prepare
- I will provide
- I will sacrifice
- I will serve
- I will speak
- I will use
- I will advance
- I will bring forth
- I will do actually
- I will take charge
- I will commit
- I will deal with
- I will vex the enemy
- I will put in execution
- I will exercise
- I will do in the widest sense
- I will fashion
- I will do surely
- I will accomplish
- I will fight man
- I will gather
- I will go about
- I will govern
- I will get

REGAL LIVING SECRET #13

MOVING OVER FOR GOD'S PERFECT ORCHESTRATION

*"I the Lord have rebuilt what was destroyed…I will **do** it." Ezekiel 36:36*

Dear King's Daughter,

Your life rests in the magnificent hands of a Master Composer and Divine Conductor. He desires to orchestrate His preordained, divine plans into your reality. *"For I know the plans I have for you," declares the Lord, "plans to prosper you and not to harm you, plans to give you hope and a future" (Jer. 29:11).* Let God be God! Would you barge into Beethoven's studio, roll up your sleeves, and start rewriting his music? Of course not. All the more with your Heavenly Father. In Ezekiel 36:36, the Lord reveals just how He will perfectly orchestrate every detail of your life. He simply says, *"I will DO it."* The Hebrew meaning of "DO" includes 80 verbs (see 36 of 80 on the left page). Isn't it amazing that a two letter verb expresses God's perfect orchestration so powerfully and extensively? So often we aren't interested in God's plan until we have created a fiasco on our own. Repent of control and trust in God's orchestration. It's never too late! God will restore and repair every mistake. Tune your heart into God's perfect will for your life. He is in the business of *"perfecting all that concerns you" (Ps. 138:17).* He will DO it!

TRADE IN:
CONTROL
taking control
of your life

TRADE UP:
TRUST
moving over for God's
perfect orchestration

▶ VIDEO:
He will DO it!

New Heart
Ginnie Johnson
Acrylic on Canvas

REGAL LIVING SECRET #14

Non-Stop Loving–In Christ

"Love your enemies, bless them that curse you, do good to them that hate you, and pray for them which despitefully use you, and persecute you; that you may be sons of your Father in heaven." Matthew 5:43-46

Dear King's Daughter,

When you truly receive God's unconditional love, you are able to give unconditional love to those around you. *"Walk in love, as Christ also has loved us and given Himself for us, an offering and a sacrifice to God for a sweet-smelling aroma" (Eph. 5:2).* Jesus taught us in word and action what unconditional love looks like in every day life. He keeps it simple in Matthew 5 (above), and so will we:

- *Love your enemies.* A King's daughter loves her enemies and does not take revenge.
- *Bless them that curse you.* A King's daughter blesses and does not curse back.
- *Do good to them that hate you.* A King's daughter does not return evil for evil.
- *Pray for them which despitefully use you.* A King's daughter prays fervently for them.
- *Pray for those who persecute you* because of Christ. A King's daughter rejoices in suffering for Christ.

Why don't we get started now? Bless someone who has offended you. Forgive someone who has mistreated you. Rely on the Holy Spirit to release Jesus' unconditional, non-stop love in and through you.

TRADE IN:
BITTERNESS
withholding love
or retaliating in anger

TRADE UP:
UNCONDITIONAL LOVE
non-stop loving
in Christ

VIDEO: New Heart

Bouquet of Blessing
Ginnie Johnson
Acrylic on Canvas

REGAL LIVING SECRET #15

OBEYING GOD'S WORD & VOICE

*"[If you] obey and do all His commandments which I command you this day....
all these blessings shall come on you, and overtake you." Deuteronomy 28:1-2*

Dear King's Daughter,

Deuteronomy 28 is a vibrant chapter in Scripture describing the outpouring of blessings on those who obey God's Word and voice. Christ's life and power in you enables you to obey. *"For it is God who works in you both to will and to do for His good pleasure" (Phil. 2:13).* The "Bouquet of Blessings" painting on the left page and the poem below are inspired by God's blessings of obedience in Deuteronomy 28.

Enjoy this Bouquet of Blessings—
A visual to remind you to receive.
God's countless, promised blessings
to those who listen and believe.

God says if you listen diligently,
Obey and do what He commands,
All these blessings will come to you,
And reach you by His loving hand.

Blessed will you be in the city
Blessed as you come and go
Blessed shall you be in your body
Blessed as your accomplishments flow

Blessed shall be your finances
Blessed in what you're called to do
Blessed because your enemies flee
Blessed with friendships, too

Blessed with the Lord's good treasure
Blessed in all the work of your hand
Blessed because you do no borrowing
Blessed and wealthy enough to lend

The Lord shall make you the head
He declares you shall not be the tail
You shall be above only—not beneath
In your kingdom destiny, you will prevail!

©Ginnie Johnson 2005

TRADE IN:
CONSEQUENCES in Deut. 28:15-68
disobeying God's
Word & voice

TRADE UP:
BLESSINGS in Deut. 28:1-14
obeying God's
Word & voice

▶ VIDEO:
Bouquets
of Blessing

MY PRAISE — Our Father who art in Heaven, Hallowed be Your Name.
Lord, I praise Your Name! (find God's Names on page 47).

HIS PLAN — Your kingdom come, Your will be done, on earth as it is in heaven.
What is Your glorious will for me in Your kingdom today?

HIS PROVISION — Give us this day our daily bread.
What do I need, Lord? Prayer Requests:

HIS PARDON OF ME — And forgive us our debts,
Lord, show me what sins to confess.

HIS PARDON THROUGH ME — As we forgive our debtors.
Lord, who do I need to forgive?

HIS PURIFICATION — And do not lead us into temptation,
Thank you God for giving me power to withstand any temptation in these areas:

HIS PROTECTION — But deliver us from the evil one.
I put on the full armor of God. I resist any attack from the devil in Jesus' Name.

HIS POWER — For Yours is the kingdom and the power and the glory forever. Amen.
How can I serve Your kingdom and live in Your power for Your glory today?

REGAL LIVING SECRET #16

Praying the Lord's Prayer

"In this manner, therefore, pray." Matthew 6:9

Dear King's Daughter,

Jesus gave us the Lord's Prayer to receive "full coverage" every day! So often we say this prayer quickly and routinely, not realizing its fullness. The Lord's Prayer gives you precision guidance to the center of God's perfect will—where you find protection, blessing, and joy *"on earth as it is in heaven."* Notice the progression in the Lord's Prayer. It starts off with praise and moves through everything you need from forgiveness to protection from the enemy (and more!). Jesus not only gave us a model of how to pray, he also showed us when to pray! *"Early in the morning, while it was still dark, He arose and went out and departed to a lonely place, and was praying there" (Mark 1:35).* If one-on-one time with God was essential for Jesus every morning, how much more should it be essential to us? Let the Lord's Prayer deepen your intimacy with God. Tell God, "I want to *know* You—not just more *know about* You or what other people know. I want to know Your heart." With a ready pen, pray daily through the Lord's Prayer line by line, receiving His thoughts for each day. Use the application questions on the left page. Trust the Lord to reveal Himself in each line of HIS prayer.

TRADE IN:
PARTIAL COVERAGE
not praying
the Lord's Prayer

TRADE UP:
FULL COVERAGE
praying the
Lord's Prayer daily

PODCAST:
"The Lord's Prayer"
by Dr. Robert Mawire

THEFT
JOHN 10:10

DEATH
JOHN 10:10

DESTRUCTION
JOHN 10:10

CONFUSION
1 COR. 14:33

DEVOURING
1 PETER 5:8

DISEASE
MATT. 10:1

HINDRANCES
1 THES. 2:18

ACCUSATIONS
REVELATION 12:10

LIES
JOHN 8:44

TEMPTATIONS
1 COR. 7:5

SPIRIT OF FEAR
2 TIM. 1:7

KINGDOM AUTHORITY STRATEGIES

1. SUBMIT TO GOD AND THE DEVIL WILL FLEE. JAMES 4:7

2. PUT ON THE FULL ARMOR OF GOD
EPHESIANS 6:10-17

3. REBUKE THE DEVIL WITH SCRIPTURE: "IT IS WRITTEN…"
MATTHEW 4:1-11

4. TELL SATAN OUT LOUD, "GO! IN JESUS' NAME"
MATTHEW 8:32

REGAL LIVING SECRET #17

QUENCHING THE ENEMY'S DARTS

"I have given you authority to overcome all the power of the enemy; nothing will harm you." Luke 10:19

Dear King's Daughter,

    You have been entrusted with the powerhouse secret of kingdom authority to quench the enemy's darts. Many Christians spend more time putting out fires from satan's darts than extinguishing them before they hit. Though the battle rages, Jesus triumphed over the enemy at the cross. The same power that raised Jesus from the dead is in you to destroy satan's work on earth (Luke 10:19). *"[Jesus] who is in you is greater than he [satan] who is in the world" (1 John 4:4).* Rise up, Christian soldier! Kingdom boot camp starts now. *"Be alert and of sober mind. Your enemy the devil prowls around like a roaring lion looking for someone to devour. Resist him, standing firm in the faith" (1 Peter 5:8).* Let's get trained in four Kingdom Authority Strategies: **1.)** Submit to God **2.)** Put on the full armor of God. *"Above all, take the shield of faith [that] quenches all the fiery darts of the wicked one" (Eph. 6:16).* **3.)** Rebuke the devil with Scripture **4.)** Tell satan out loud, "Go in Jesus' Name." Be aware of the enemy's darts so that you can cancel attacks before they wreak hellish havoc. *"No weapon formed against you shall prosper" (Isa. 54:17).* Let the Holy Spirit continue to build you up in kingdom authority by looking up the verses on the left page in your Bible. You are not a victim. You are a victor in Christ.

TRADE IN:
VICTIM MINDSET
tolerating satan's darts
in your life and others'

TRADE UP:
VICTOR MINDSET
quenching the enemy's darts
with kingdom authority

SARAH'S SONG:
You There

WITH GOD

But Jesus looked at them and said,
"With men it is impossible, but not with God;
for with God all things are possible." (Matthew 19:26)
With God all things are possible—nothing too big, nothing too small.
With God, there is no problem too big to solve. (Ps. 138:8)
With God, there is no disease too severe to heal. (Isa. 53:45)
With God, there is no destiny too difficult to unfold. (Jer. 29:11)
With God, there is no family too broken to mend. (Gen. 12:3)
With God, there is no relationship too difficult to reunite. (Deut. 28:2)
With God, there is no mystery too difficult to understand. (1 Cor 2:7-10)
With God, there is no job too hard to find. (Deut. 28:12)
With God, there is no wealth too difficult to receive. (Deut. 8:18)
With God, there is no request too trivial to ask. (John 14:14)
With God, there is no trial too big to finish. (Jas. 1:2-14)
With God, there is no person's soul too tormented to make whole. (1 John 4:18)
With God, there is no habit too hard to break. (Rom. 8:15, 21)
With God, there is no sin too big to cover. (1 Peter 4:8)
With God, there is no task too difficult to start. (Gen. 18:14)
With God, there is no devil too big to conquer. (1 John 4:4)
With God, there is no mistake too big to forgive. (1 John 1:9)
With God, there is no desire too unique to fulfill. (Ps. 37:4)
With God, there is no memory too traumatic to erase. (Isa. 43:18-19)
With God, there is no missed opportunity too late to redeem. (Isa. 50:2)
With God, there is no person too difficult to save. (Matt. 18:12-14)
"With God," all things are possible for you

"With God" is the answer!

© Ginnie Johnson 2010

REGAL LIVING SECRET #18

REJOICING IN TRIALS BY FAITH

*"My brethren, count it all joy when you fall into various trials, knowing that the testing of your **faith** produces patience. But let patience have its perfect work, that you may be perfect and complete, lacking nothing." James 1:2-4*

Dear King's Daughter,

One of the most important trademarks of a King's daughter is rejoicing! Rejoicing in trials expresses to God that you trust Him and that you are willing to be matured in an area this trial is revealing. Trials will come. Pass every test with flying colors by rejoicing by faith at all times, in all circumstances, and in all places. *"Rejoice in the Lord **always**. I will say it again: Rejoice!" (Phil. 4:4)*. God will honor your sacrifice of praise and give you patience. Patience will do its perfect work so that you will be mature and complete, lacking nothing. Sounds like a kingdom deal! You can worship or wallow. Rejoice in trials by faith and receive hope—or complain and stay stuck in hopelessness. **Make a choice to rejoice.** *"Be joyful always; pray continually; give thanks in all circumstances, for this is God's will for you in Christ Jesus" (1 Thes. 5:16-18)*. Shout the "With God" cheer on the left page BY FAITH! Go ahead and get some pom-poms out or put your hair in a high pony tail (who doesn't need some humor in the middle of a trial?). *"With God, all things are possible" (Matt. 19:26)*. All things means all things!

TRADE IN:	TRADE UP:
HOPELESSNESS	HOPE & FAITH
wallowing in your trials	rejoicing in your trials by faith

SARAH'S SONG:
Bless Your Name

PLANTING WEEDS | PLANTING SEEDS

I will never find a job. I hate my job.	Thank you that God knows the plans He has for me (Jer. 29:11).
I will never get better or recover. Why did God do this to me?	Thank you that by His stripes I am healed (Isa. 53:5).
I am not good at / I can't _____. I will never be able to _____.	Thank you that I can do all things through Christ who strengthens me! (Phil. 4:13).
I do not like the way I look. I will never be as pretty as she is.	Thank you that I am fearfully and wonderfully made! (Ps. 139:13-14).
I will never have a boyfriend or husband. Does God have anyone for me?	Thank you that God does not withhold anything good from me (Psalm 84:11).
I will always struggle with this sin. This temptation is too strong.	Thank you that I walk not in the flesh but in the Spirit (Rom. 8:9).
My marriage is failing.	Thank you that what God has joined together, man will not separate. (Mark 10:9).

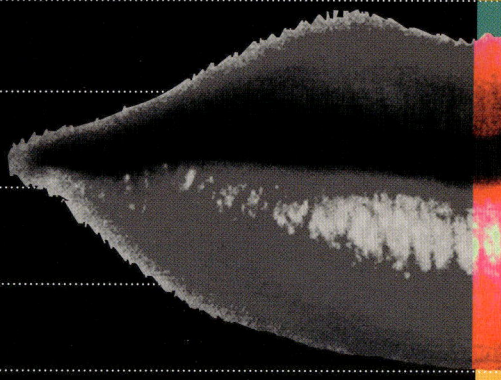

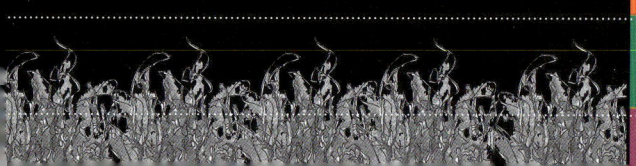

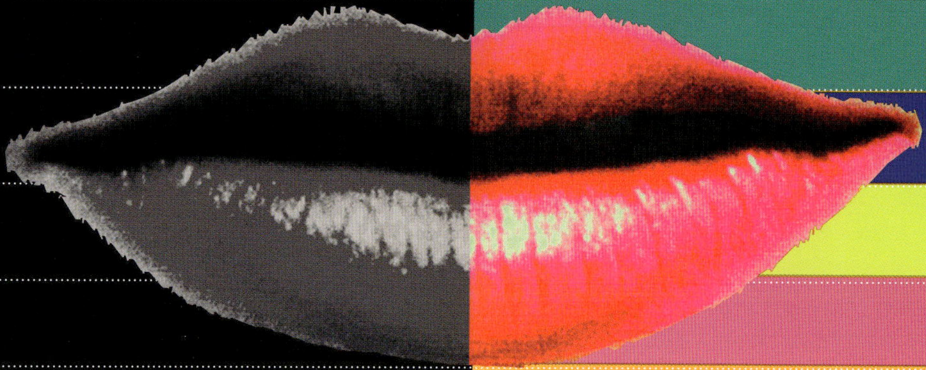

REGAL LIVING SECRET #19

SPEAKING GOD'S PROMISES

"Out of the same mouth proceed blessing and cursing. These things should not be so." James 3:10

Dear King's Daughter,

Did you know there is supernatural power in every word that comes out of your mouth? *"The tongue has the power of life and death" (Prov. 18:21).* Negative words of doubt, fear, and unbelief can curse situations, people, and your life. On the other hand, speaking promises from the Bible brings powerful blessings to situations, people, and your life. *"Out of the same mouth proceed blessing and cursing. These things should not be so" (James 3:10).* God's promises are anything He says in His Word that reveals His perfect will for you. The Lord says, *"I am ready to perform My Word" (Jer 1:12).* Your Father has never broken a promise and He won't start with you. He says *"My Word that goes out from My mouth; It will not return to Me empty, but will accomplish what I desire" (Isa. 55:11).* Instead of planting weeds with your words, plant seeds of God's promises from the Bible! *"For all the promises of God in Him are Yes, and in Him Amen, to the glory of God through us" (2 Cor. 1:20).* Studies show women speak about 20,000 words a day.* Think about 20,000 seeds of God's promises planted in your life and the lives of others every day. Oh the glorious potential! By faith, put "thank you" in front of the promise you need.

*Louann Brizendine, The Female Brain

TRADE IN: NEGATIVE WORDS	TRADE UP: GOD'S PROMISES
speaking weeds of problems	speaking seeds of God's promises

SARAH'S SONG: Promises

Lost & Found
Ginnie Johnson
Mixed Media

REGAL LIVING SECRET #20

THANKING JESUS
FOR HIS FINISHED WORK OF THE CROSS

*"Surely [Jesus] has **borne** our griefs and **carried** our sorrows...He was **wounded** for our transgressions, He was **bruised** for our iniquities; The chastisement for our peace was upon Him and by His stripes we are **healed**." Isaiah 53:4-5*

Dear King's Daughter,

Let's shout from the rooftops that JESUS STILL HEALS! Read Isaiah 53:4-5 above to get your mind renewed on the finished work of the cross (notice the bold past tense verbs). Jesus' death and resurrection conquered every power of darkness 2,000 years ago. *"By His stripes we are healed"* spiritually, emotionally, and physically. Jesus said, *"It is finished!" (John 19:30).* Jesus has **borne** your grief. Why bear it too? Jesus has **carried** your sorrow. Why carry it too? Jesus was **wounded** for your transgressions. Why be wounded too? He was **bruised** for your iniquities. Why be bruised too? Whatever you are experiencing, Jesus already took it on! His blood has paid the price for your complete healing. Start thanking Jesus for the finished work of the cross—even if it is in advance. God desires that His children live whole and healed. *"Beloved, I pray that in all respects you may prosper and be in good health, just as your soul prospers" (3 John 1:2).* Also find "kingdom instructions" to pray for healing in James 5:14-16. Here is a preview: *"Confess your sins to one another, and pray for one another, that you may be healed."*

TRADE IN:	TRADE UP:
ISSUES & ILLNESS	HEALING
not receiving Jesus' finished work of the cross	thanking Jesus for His finished work of the cross

♪ SARAH'S SONG
Thank You for the Cross

One New Man
Ginnie Johnson
Mixed Media

REGAL LIVING SECRET #21

Understanding
THE MYSTERY OF ISRAEL

"I will bless those that bless you. I will curse those that curse you." Genesis 12:3

Dear King's Daughter,

This next secret might be the most powerful, yet puzzling, piece to living regally in reality. As a Christian, you are a branch connected to the roots of Israel. The King has never stopped cherishing Israel as His chosen people and wants you to share His same compassion and love for her. Paul warns, *"Do not boast against the branches...remember that you do not support the root, but the root supports you. I do not desire that you be ignorant of this mystery"* (Rom. 11:18, 25). The covenant God made with Abraham, the father of Israel, still stands today: *"I will bless those that bless you. I will curse those that curse you"* (Gen 12:3). God invites us to share His heart for Israel. *"Pray for the peace (shalom) of Jerusalem; they that love her shall prosper"* (Ps. 122:6). As Israel comes under terrorist attacks, anti-Semitism and international pressure to divide her land, we are called to stand with her. *"For whoever touches Israel touches the apple of God's eye"* (Zech. 2:8). The Lord also wants us to give to Israel. *"For if the Gentiles have been partakers of their spiritual things, their duty is also to minister to them in material things"* (Rom. 15:27)*. Align yourself with God's heart and pray for the peace of Jerusalem right now!

TRADE IN:
IGNORANCE
ignoring or cursing Israel

TRADE UP:
GOD'S HEART FOR ISRAEL
understanding the
mystery of Israel

SARAH'S SONG:
Peace Over You

*Join King's Daughters in giving to Israel. See Page 87

UNDERSTANDING THE MYSTERY OF ISRAEL

Ginnie in Israel, 1996

PERSONAL STORY FROM GINNIE

In August of 1996, The Lord clearly spoke to me, "I want you to go to Israel and pray through the land." I thought, "Why Israel?" so I went to the Word. I randomly flipped open my Bible. Out of all Scripture, I turned to Psalm 122:6. *"Pray for the peace of Jerusalem: they shall prosper that love her."* God supernaturally confirmed His voice. I said to God, "I have never thought of praying for Israel. **I need You to pray through me."**

Just three weeks later, I was in Israel praying through the land! The entire trip, my left side was physically burning. At the time, I thought I was being healed of a recently diagnosed breast tumor. But when I got home, I still had to have the benign tumor removed. So I asked the Lord, "What was that burning on my left side? I thought you were healing that tumor." God replied, "Ginnie, when you pray for Israel, it's like Drano® (strong drain pipe cleaner) pouring over your heart. I was getting rid of all the built-up plaque of sin and old habits. I was healing your heart." Incredible! Praying for Israel had brought a new purity to my heart.

A month later, I offered to take my three daughters ice skating after they cleaned their rooms. I went to check on Sarah, who was eight years old at the time, and found her sitting at her desk writing. "Sarah, you are supposed to be cleaning your room!" I exclaimed. I walked over to see what she was writing and saw the words: *"Today is the day we will kneel and pray, praying for the peace of Jerusalem! You say those that love her will prosper. Praying for the peace of Jerusalem!"* I could not believe my eyes. Sarah was writing a song for Israel. I said, "Sarah, don't move. Keep writing. I will clean your room for you."

As I picked up her clothes, toys, and shoes, the Lord spoke to me, "Just as you are putting Sarah's messy room in order for her as she prays for the peace of Jerusalem, I will put your life in divine order and divine blessing as you pray for My people. I will do it for you!" At the time, I was in desperate need for His restoration! As I prayed for the peace of Jerusalem, I saw God fulfill His promise. God restored divine order and blessing in every area of my life. Years later, God continues to fulfill His Psalm 122:6 promise for me and my family! As I pray for Israel's shalom (peace), He gives me shalom (peace). As I bless Israel financially, He blesses me financially. As I prayer for her prosperity, He prospers me. But don't just take my word for it. Bless Israel and watch the Lord fulfill His promise and perform His Word in your life.

Ginnie & Sarah in Israel, 2011

PERSONAL STORY FROM SARAH

I very clearly remember the day I wrote my first song for Israel (pictured). I was sitting at my little desk receiving the words and melody from the Lord. What a powerful moment! God was giving me a heart for Israel at eight years old.

In 2011, I had the joy of visiting Israel with my mom. We walked where Abraham, David, Jesus, and the disciples walked. We toured sites where biblical history was made and end time prophesies are going to be fulfilled—an incredible juxtaposition of past, present, and future. During the trip, the Lord gave me "Peace Over You," a new song for Israel. I sang the chorus over the land: *"We pray peace over you / Nothing broken, nothing bruised / shattered pieces whole again / missing parts found in Yeshua"*

One night, I was praying for Israel before I fell asleep and started to hear my heartbeat. Every heartbeat resounded through my entire body. I had never experienced anything like it! I asked the Lord, "What are You telling me?" I heard Him say, "This is my heart for Israel. My heart beats for her." Thank you, Holy Spirit, for revealing such an intimate spot of God's heart to me! Ask the Lord to give you a heart for Israel. Experience the power of this mystery.

Sarah's original song for Israel at 8 years old

If you are looking for a way to give to Israel, we invite you to join *King's Daughters* in supporting The Ariel Warm Home, a multi-dimensional community enrichment center, which provides teenagers and families with new opportunities to succeed in life. Read more about The Ariel Warm Home on page 87 or on our website under "causes." www.kings-daughters.com

THE PROVERBS 31 WOMAN

Christ-Centered	10 Who can find a virtuous woman? For her worth is far above rubies.
Cooperative	11 The heart of her husband safely trusts her; so he will have no lack of gain.
Constant	12 She does him good and not evil all the days of her life.
Compliant	13 She seeks wool and flax, and willingly works with her hands.
Culinary	14 She is like the merchant ships, she brings her food from afar.
Considerate	15 She also rises while it is yet night, and provides food for her household, and a portion for her maidservants.
Clever	16 She considers a field and buys it; from her profits she plants a vineyard.
Committed	17 She girds herself with strength, and strengthens her arms.
Confident	18 She perceives that her merchandise is good, and her lamp does not go out by night.
Creative	19 She stretches out her hands to the distaff, and her hand holds the spindle.
Compassionate	20 She extends her hand to the poor, yes, she reaches out her hands to the needy.
Certain	21 She is not afraid of snow for her household, for all her household is clothed with scarlet.
Clothed well	22 She makes tapestry for herself; her clothing is fine linen and purple.
Congratulatory	23 Her husband is known in the gates, when he sits among the elders of the land.
Commercial	24 She makes linen garments and sells them, and supplies sashes for the merchants.
Celebratory	25 Strength and honor are her clothing; she shall rejoice in time to come.
Cheerful	26 She opens her mouth with wisdom, and on her tongue is the law of kindness.
Circumspect	27 She watches over the ways of her household, and does not eat the bread of idleness.
Cherished	28 Her children rise up and call her blessed; her husband also, and he praises her:
Competent	29 Many daughters have done well, but you excel them all.
Complimented	30 Charm is deceitful and beauty is passing,
Commended	31 But a woman who fears the Lord, she shall be praised.

REGAL LIVING SECRET #22

VALUING GODLY WOMANHOOD

"Who can find a virtuous woman? For her price is far above rubies." Proverbs 31:10-31

Dear King's Daughter,

When God created woman, He had big plans! He formed women to be multifaceted and multitalented—with multiple roles. God gives us His divinely inspired idea for womanhood with the Proverbs 31 Woman. She is not outdated, stereotypical, nor confined to the kitchen. She stands as a pillar of strength. Her value exceeds the cost of rubies. She is a vibrant woman of practical breadth and spiritual character. God's presence shines in her character, relationships, and work. Flawed messages about womanhood flood our culture and worldly womanhood has emerged. A worldly woman confuses sexuality for femininity. She values vanity over virtue. She would rather dominate men than respect them. She disdains domestic roles as old-fashioned stereotypes. Joyfully let Christ give you power to be a vibrant Proverbs 31 woman! Look at the pillar of her characteristics on the left. Personalize each verse with your name. She is you, by faith! *"Many daughters have done well, but you [will] excel them all" (Prov. 31:29).* Allow the Proverbs 31 Woman to be your mentor. Her kingdom advice covers business, home life, relationships, and even outer beauty! Sit down and have a cup of coffee with her once a month for a refreshing reminder of God's plan for you as a virtuous woman.

TRADE IN:	TRADE UP:
VANITY	VIRTUE
prioritizing worldly womanhood	valuing godly womanhood

VIDEO: A Pillar of Strength

Colors of Praise
Ginnie Johnson
Acrylic on Canvas

REGAL LIVING SECRET #23

Worshipping God

*"Oh come, let us **sing** to the Lord! Let us **shout joyfully** to the Rock of our salvation.
Let us **come before His presence with thanksgiving**; Let us **shout joyfully to Him with psalms**.
For the Lord is the great God, and the great King above all gods...
Oh come, let us **worship** and **bow down**; Let us **kneel** before the Lord our Maker." Psalm 95:1-3,6*

Dear King's Daughter,

Let us magnify the Lord! Let us exalt His Name together! He is holy, perfect, and worthy of our praise! He is mighty in power, rich in mercy, and abounding in love. He is good all the time. Doesn't that lift your spirit? Worship invites God's presence into your life—and *"in God's presence is fullness of joy and pleasures forever more" (Ps. 16:11)*. You were created to be a worshipper. Worship takes your eyes off worldly circumstances and fixes them on Jesus. Confusion, stress, and depression flee as you behold God's goodness and enter into His presence. God *"inhabits the praises of [His people]" (Ps. 22:3)*. As you worship God, He pours out revelation, strength, intimacy, and transformation. *"We all, with unveiled face, beholding the glory of the Lord, are being transformed into the same image from one degree of glory to another" (2 Cor. 3:18)*. He loves to be worshipped, adored, and praised. He is worthy! Read Psalm 95 above and be ignited to worship the Lord at all times, in every way. If you ever feel anxious or depressed, read Psalms 145-150 OUT LOUD! Receive fullness of joy as you agree with the truth of who God is.

TRADE IN:
DEPRESSION & WORRY
worrying about circumstances

TRADE UP:
FULLNESS OF JOY
worshipping God

SARAH'S SONG:
Burning Heart

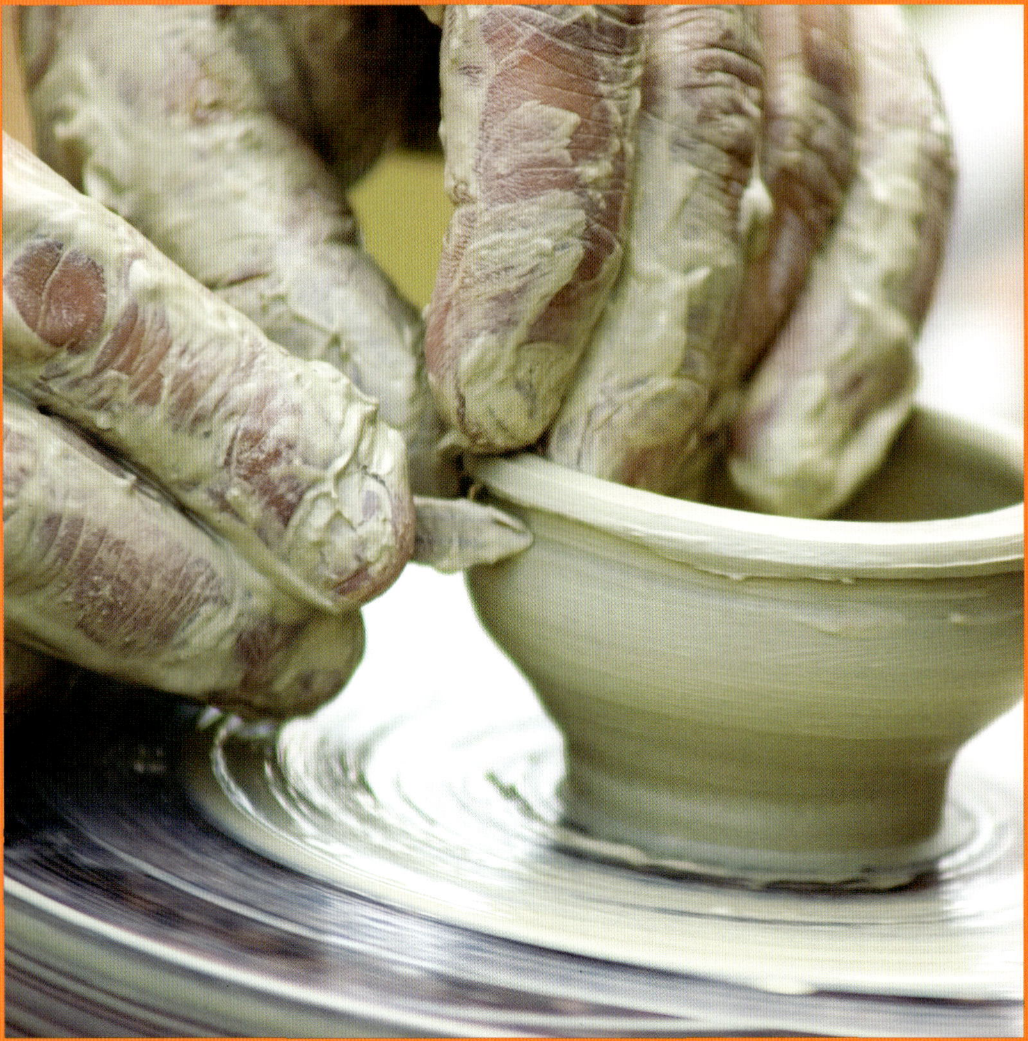

REGAL LIVING SECRET #24

"X-PRESSING" HIS WORKMANSHIP

*"For we are His **workmanship**, created in Christ Jesus unto good works, which God preordained that we should walk in them!" Ephesians 2:10*

Dear King's Daughter,

No one on earth is made just like you! You are designed for a unique kingdom destiny that will glorify God, meet needs, and simultaneously delight your heart. Your Creator gave you spiritual gifts, practical talents, and even physical attributes to fulfill His calling on your life. You are HIS workmanship—on HIS timetable—walking in HIS destiny for you. It is not up to you (nor anyone else) to plan out your own works, your own timetable, and your own destiny. God desires for you to surrender to His divine plan and let Him take care of the rest. *"Offer your bodies as a living sacrifice, holy and pleasing to God—this is your true and proper worship" (Rom. 12:1).* His preordained good works follow worship. Put works before worship and you are in for a long road of exhaustion, ambition, and dead-end plans. *"We are the clay, You are the Potter; we are all the work of Your hand" (Isaiah 64:8).* He is the Potter and you are the clay. Stay on His wheel and let Him shape you into your full kingdom potential. *"He who has begun a good work in you will complete it until the day of Jesus Christ" (Phil. 1:6).*

TRADE IN:	TRADE UP:
YOUR WORKS	HIS WORKS
following your own ambitions	expressing His workmanship

SARAH'S SONG: Footsteps

Be available for God's divine appointments wherever you go....

- class
- the grocery store
- luncheons
- the gym
- meetings
- parties
- at work
- on vacation
- out & about
- at home
- even on a rainy day!
- errands
- social events
- mission trips

"How beautiful...are the feet of her who brings good news." Isaiah 52:7

REGAL LIVING SECRET #25

YIELDING TO DIVINE APPOINTMENTS

"How beautiful upon the mountains are the feet of him who brings good news, who proclaims peace, who brings glad tidings of good things, who proclaims salvation." Isaiah 52:7

Dear King's Daughter,

Divine appointments are part of a King's daughter's daily kingdom destiny. She yields to the Holy Spirit's prompting for conversations, prayers, words of encouragement, or thoughtful deeds for the people around her. Her time, talents, and treasures are from God and for His glory. This is your calling in Christ! God's divine appointments are as subtle as a short encouragement and as bold as a prayer for healing or deliverance. There can be a very small window of opportunity to obey. Respond quickly to the Holy Spirit! Will your friends or family be confused at your peculiar ways? Yes. Will people experience the love of God or hear the gospel for the first time? Yes and Hallelujah! Do not let fear, unavailability, nor reluctance cause you the disappointment of missing a divine appointment. Let Isaiah 52:7 ignite you for divine appointments wherever you go: *"How beautiful upon the mountains are the feet of him who **brings good news**, who **proclaims peace**, who **brings glad tidings** of good things, who **proclaims salvation**, who **says to Zion, 'Your God reigns!'"*** You will never regret yielding to the Holy Spirit's leading—ever!

TRADE IN: DISAPPOINTMENTS	TRADE UP: DIVINE APPOINTMENTS
missing God's divine appointments	yielding to God's divine appointments

VIDEO: Divine Opportunities

Greater Works
Sarah Johnson
Acrylic on Canvas

"The colored circles represent people of all generations who are walking in greater works."

REGAL LIVING SECRET #26

ZEALOUSLY DOING GREATER WORKS

*"Most assuredly, I say to you, who believe in Me, the works that I do they will do also; and **greater work**s than these they will do, because I go to My Father." John 14:12*

Dear King's Daughter,

We trust you have enjoyed trading up to living regally in reality, secret by secret! *"Freely you have received; freely give" (Matt. 10:8).* The works Jesus did, He calls you to do also. *"As Jesus is, so are [you] in this world" (1 John 4:17).* In fact, Jesus is praying for you to do even greater works than Him *(John 14:12)*. "Greater works" is not a figure of speech—it is the reality of your calling. In Jesus' name, cancel the devil's accusations that you don't have enough time, talent, or resources to be about the King's business. You are a prayed-up, traded-up King's daughter. You are made for God's greater works and equipped in His power. You are so filled with God's love that it overflows to your family, friends, community, and the nations. You have been given the fullness of Jesus Christ in you to bring God's glory to the earth (Isa. 60:1). Adopt Jesus' mission statement as your own. *"The Spirit of the LORD is upon Me, because He has anointed Me to preach the gospel to the meek; He has sent Me to heal the brokenhearted, to proclaim liberty to the captives and recovery of sight to the blind, to set at liberty those who are oppressed" (Luke 4:18).* King's daughter—zealously go forth to the lost, hurting, broken, and sick. The world is waiting!

TRADE IN: BUSYNESS	TRADE UP: GREATER WORKS
missing out on greater works	zealously doing greater works

SARAH'S SONG: Walk on Water

REGAL LIVING SECRETS • A–Z

		Trade In	Trade Up
Secret #1:	**A**ccepting God's Perfect Love	FEAR	PERFECT LOVE
Secret #2:	**B**eginning Your Day with Abba	PERFORMANCE	RELATIONSHIP
Secret #3:	**C**elebrating at the Father's Party	REBELLION OR PRIDE	HUMILITY
Secret #4:	**D**eclaring Christ in You	OLD MAN	NEW CREATION
Secret #5:	**E**xpressing Christ through You	SELF-EFFORT	FAITH
Secret #6:	**F**inding Security in Christ	INSECURITY & SORROW	SECURITY & RADIANCE
Secret #7:	**G**oing to God's Word	FOOLISHNESS	WISDOM
Secret #8:	**H**earing God's Voice	MY WILL	GOD'S WILL
Secret #9:	**I**nterceding For & With Others	INTERFERENCE	INTERCESSION
Secret #10:	**J**oyfully Receiving Abundant Life	HELL ON EARTH	HEAVEN ON EARTH
Secret #11:	**K**nowing God's Names	LACK	TOTAL PROVISION
Secret #12:	**L**iving in the Holy Spirit's Power	POWERLESSNESS	POWER
Secret #13:	**M**oving Over for God's Orchestration	CONTROL	TRUST
Secret #14:	**N**on-Stop Loving in Christ	BITTERNESS	UNCONDITIONAL LOVE
Secret #15:	**O**beying God's Word & Voice	CONSEQUENCES	BLESSINGS
Secret #16:	**P**raying the Lord's Prayer	PARTIAL COVERAGE	FULL COVERAGE
Secret #17:	**Q**uenching the enemy's Darts	VICTIM MIND-SET	VICTOR MIND-SET
Secret #18:	**R**ejoicing in Trials by Faith	HOPELESSNESS	HOPE & FAITH
Secret #19:	**S**peaking God's Promises	NEGATIVE WORDS	GOD'S PROMISES
Secret #20:	**T**hanking Jesus for His Finished Work of the Cross	ISSUES & ILLNESS	HEALING
Secret #21:	**U**nderstanding the Mystery of Israel	IGNORANCE	GOD'S HEART FOR ISRAEL
Secret #22:	**V**aluing Godly Womanhood	VANITY	VIRTUE
Secret #23:	**W**orshipping God	DEPRESSION & WORRY	FULLNESS OF JOY
Secret #24:	**"X**-pressing" God's Workmanship	MY WORKS	HIS WORKS
Secret #25:	**Y**ielding to Divine Appointments	DISAPPOINTMENTS	DIVINE APPOINTMENTS
Secret #26:	**Z**ealously Doing Greater Works	BUSYNESS	GREATER WORKS

BONUS REGAL LIVING SECRET

Preparing for Jesus' Return

*"Then I heard something like the voice of a great multitude and like the sound of many waters and like the sound of mighty peals of thunder, saying, "Hallelujah! For the Lord our God, the Almighty, reigns. "Let us rejoice and be glad and give the glory to Him, for the marriage of the Lamb has come and **His bride has made herself ready."** It was given to her to clothe herself in fine linen, bright and clean; for the fine linen is the righteous acts of the saints" (Rev. 19:6-8).*

We believe the hour is late and time is short.
The bride makes herself ready!
Trade In and Trade Up until Jesus' return.
He is coming back for a pure and spotless bride.
"The King's Daughter is all glorious within" (Ps. 45:13).

VIDEO:
Closing Prayer
for You

Prayer of Salvation

Jesus Christ has invited *"whosoever believes in Him" (John 3:16)* to become a member of His royal family! *"If you confess with your mouth the Lord Jesus and believe in your heart that God has raised Him from the dead, you will be saved" (Rom. 10:9)*. Below is a prayer to receive Jesus Christ as your Savior and Lord. Today, you could begin an abiding relationship with Him on earth and live with assurance of eternity in heaven! Abundant life in Christ is about to be yours! *"For God so loved the world that He gave His only begotten Son, that whosoever believes in Him shall not perish but have everlasting life" (John 3:16)*.

Dear Lord, I recognize that I am a sinner in need of the salvation You offer through believing in Your Son, Jesus Christ. I repent of my sin and receive Your forgiveness. Please come into my heart as my Lord and Savior. I am ready to become a royal King's daughter *"all glorious within!" (Psalm 45:11)*. Thank You that I now live led by Your Spirit and instructed in Your Word. I praise You for a new beginning to live in You, with You, and through You from this day forward. In Jesus' Name, Amen.

Many Thanks!

From Ginnie & Sarah: First and foremost, we give praise, honor and thanksgiving to the King. Thank you for giving us abundant life through Jesus. Thank you for our identity and inheritance as King's daughters. A MILLION thanks to our editing team! Thank you to Pastor Jim Borchert for your oversight and editing of *Trading Up* to ensure sound doctrine and biblical accuracy. Jennie Gilchrist, Wynette Kent, Nancy Rudd, Cristin Parker, Nan Kirchhofer, Laura Lodwick, Elizabeth Emerson, Lissie Donosky, Dan Stephens, Roxanne Sheehan, Elisabeth Jordan, Barbi Townsend, Beverly Hensley, Lucy Guerriero, Elizabeth Kadine, and Liz Case Pickens. Your excellence, wisdom and kindness have fueled *Trading Up for a King's Daughter* to the finish line. We are so grateful for your feedback and cheerleading every step along the way! Countless thanks to Wayne Johnson, a loving husband and father! Thank you Elizabeth Johnson and Caroline Johnson for your encouraging notes and prayers!

From Ginnie: Thank you Pastor Jim Borchert for your anointed teaching over the last 22 years. Your message of rest, relationship with God, rejoicing, and repenting is preparing the bride. Thank you Dr. Robert Mawire for igniting me for 22 years! I have been brought up and blessed in my regal privilege as a "King's Kid." I have also been blessed by your precious wife and ministry partner, Janet. What a blessing to sow into your ministry. Thank you Elizabeth Robinson for answering the Lord's call to bring me the verse that was a "kingdom catalyst" in my destiny as a King's daughter. Thank you Sarah Johnson for coming alongside me in this King's Daughters vision. Walking alongside you in ministry is a treasure and privilege.

From Sarah: Thank you Mom for teaching me to be a King's daughter. Your creativity and perseverance are an inspiration. Thank you Dr. Robert Mawire for your teaching, prayers, and wisdom! God has used you powerfully to ignite me with a Kingdom mind-set and identity. Thank you to my family and friends for all your incredible support and encouragement!

KING'S DAUGHTERS
CAUSES

Proceeds from King's Daughters benefit:

THE ARIEL WARM HOME IN ISRAEL

The Ariel Warm Home is a multi-dimensional community enrichment center, which provides teenagers and families with new opportunities to succeed in life. Services include counseling, skills training, and Torah studies for at-risk teenage girls. Ginnie has been involved with the city of Ariel for 18 years and developed a close relationship with the city's founder and mayor, the late Ron Nachman and his wife Dorith. In 2011, Ginnie and Sarah visited the Nachmans in Ariel to find an Israeli cause for King's Daughters (pictured). They helped launch The Ariel Warm Home and are honored to be a part of its growth.

WRNO WORLDWIDE RADIO

Dr. Robert Mawire is a beloved pastor, internationally acclaimed author, speaker, and advisor to many world leaders. We are grateful for His kingdom teaching that has blessed our lives immensely for two decades. His books proclaim truth and ignite readers with the urgency of the hour, with titles including *America's Manifest Destiny*, *The Global Dilemma of the Final Destiny of Israel*, and *The Chronogram Code*. Dr. Mawire is heavily involved in advising Israeli leaders and opened the door for King's Daughters to have a cause in Israel (see above). Dr. Mawire and his wife, Janet, run WRNO Worldwide, a short wave and online radio station that broadcasts the gospel of Jesus Christ to the nations. **Make sure to listen to Dr. Mawire's powerful Lord's Prayer podcast (see page 61).**

MORE INFORMATION ONLINE

We would LOVE to keep celebrating you!

- Read our weekly Regal Blog.

- Send us your prayer requests, *Trading Up* testimonies, & feedback.

- Like King's Daughters on Facebook for updates & inspiration.

- Follow @kingsdaughterscelebrate on Instagram for "insta-blessings."

www.kings-daughters.com

TRADING UP APPENDIX

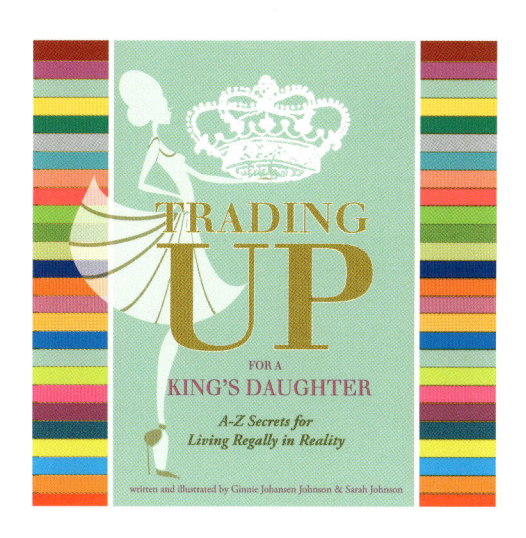

APPENDIX

Ginnie's *Trading Up* Story..90
Sarah's *Trading Up* Story..92
Sarah's Music for *Trading Up*...93
Need a Speaker?..94
Your *Trading Up* Regal Celebration... 96
Trading Up for Small Group Bible Studies.. 97
King's Daughters Art & Gift Collection... 99

TRADING UP APPENDIX

GINNIE'S *TRADING UP* STORY

Ginnie's trade up from a stressed high achiever to the happiest receiver!

People Magazine, 1979

Ginnie with President Ronald Reagan, receiving the Small Business Award.

Full time motherhood after retirement from fashion

Trading Up for a King's Daughter is my "thank you note" to the King. I stand in awe and wonder of our glorious King, who delivered me from the bondage of performance and lavished me with His love. He gave me each regal living secret—freely, kindly, creatively, and abundantly! Praise God for His relentless pursuit to rescue a stressed out high achiever and transform me into one of the happiest receivers in town!

I grew up in a performance-driven home, working for my parents' approval with good manners, good behavior, good grades, and a good, clean room. When I became a Christian at 15 years old, I strove to be a good Christian, trying to achieve a connection with God through good works (good grief!).

My freshman year of college, I started a successful fashion company, Ginnie Johansen Designs. I was propelled into the world of design, travel, awards, wealth, and popularity. Though I was saved, I found my identity in my success. I met and married my college sweetheart, Wayne, and we had our first daughter Elizabeth. When I was pregnant with our second daughter, Sarah, the Lord spoke to me and said, "I want you to retire from business and raise the next generation." I mustered the words, "Lord, I will obey you, but I need you to replace everything I am leaving with You."

After my retirement and the birth of our third daughter, Caroline, an identity crisis hit. Though I was trying my hardest to be a good wife, good mother to three girls, good friend, good homemaker, and good Christian—my best performance was failing! I was uptight, insecure, controlling, needy, exhausted, and miserable. I cried out, "Lord! I'm a CHRISTIAN! Isn't life supposed to be better than this?"

On November 7, 1996, the King answered the cry of my heart by sending His regal ambassador and my dear friend, Elizabeth Robinson. She handed me a little note and said, "Ginnie, the Lord gave me this verse for you." The note said, *"The King's daughter is all glorious within" (Psalm 45:13).* As I read the verse out loud, I was suddenly ignited in my royal position in Christ as a King's daughter. I immediately went home and soaked in the whole chapter of Psalm 45. My life was changed forever the day I realized I was the King's royalty.

A few days later, I heard these precious words from the King: "Come to My throne every day and spend 70 minutes in My presence. You need an intimate relationship with Me." Something clicked. The Lord just wanted a relationship with me, His King's daughter. A relationship—not my works nor my best efforts. In spite of my struggles and frustrations, He just wanted ME! So every morning, I got up and spent 70 minutes in my favorite chair (see the meaning of 70 to the right). As I read the Word, prayed, and listened to worship music, I began to experience an abiding relationship with God for the first time. Just as the father embraced his prodigal son returning home, so my Heavenly Father held me in His arms and celebrated me as His regal heir. My quiet times changed from duty to delight!

During my "throne time," the King delivered me from the stress of performance that entangled me for 21 years of being a Christian. He opened my eyes to see I was not **hired** to achieve for Him, but made a **heir** to receive *"every good and perfect gift from above" (James 1:17).* As I received, God removed areas of sin and disorder. I started to **TRADE IN** every area of bondage to the world, the flesh and the devil and **TRADE UP** to divine order and divine blessing in Christ. Like Eliza Doolittle from *My Fair Lady*, the King began a "regal lifestyle makeover" and taught me to think, speak, and live like a King's daughter. Each Regal Living Secret in *Trading Up for a King's Daughter* is inspired from a real encounter with the Lord.

Your own trading up story will be wonderfully unique. The King knows what you need and how you will best receive each Regal Living Secret. He desires that you live in an abiding relationship with Him. Repent where He leads you to repent and receive ALL that He wants you to receive. Hear the King say to you, "King's daughter, come celebrate at My throne (Luke 15:23). *"ALL that I have is yours" (Luke 15:31).*

The purpose of writing *Trading Up "is to do the will of Him who sent me, and to finish His work" (John 4:34).* Sarah and I pray that you receive the abundant life Jesus offers *"on earth as it is in heaven" (Matt. 6:10).* Let's Celebrate!

—*Ginnie Johnson*

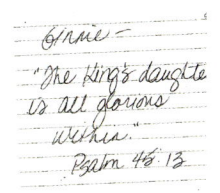

The life-changing note

Ginnie's favorite quiet time chair

70
God showed me why He wanted me to spend 70 minutes at His throne. The numeric meaning of 70 in Hebrew is perfect spiritual order carried out with all spiritual power.

Ginnie with husband, Wayne, and three daughters (left to right) Caroline, Elizabeth & Sarah

TRADING UP APPENDIX

SARAH'S *TRADING UP* STORY

Sarah's trade up to God's handpicked destiny for her life!

My testimony is a story of God's faithfulness in my life. From day one, the Lord has been pursing my heart to *know* Him more, not just *know about* Him. He daily draws me to enjoy a close relationship with Him and refuse any tendency to try to be a "good Christian girl."

I became a Christian at 4 years old. I grew up in a Christian home with a steadfast father, creative mother, two fun sisters, and wonderful friends. I was continually taught God's Word and about His love for me. What a huge gift!

My senior year at the University of Texas, God spoke to me, "Go back to Dallas and I will send you all over the world." Though I had plans to go anywhere *but* Dallas to start my news reporting career, I obeyed God. While in Dallas, the Lord put on my heart to help my mom write *Trading Up for a King's Daughter*—a book she envisioned for years. Our "fun summer project" turned into my calling.

As I studied God's Word and wrote *Trading Up for a King's Daughter*, the Lord gave me songs that complement the chapters of our book. I do not call myself a songwriter. I am a song receiver! Each song echoes my prayers to the Lord or His voice to me. My hope is that listeners make the lyrics their prayer to the Lord and hear Him speaking to their heart.

My life has not been perfect. I make mistakes and experience seasons of doubt. Daily repentance and confession are necessary in my life. But my story is not about me. My story is about a faithful Father who keeps pursuing my heart, a Savior who rescued me from darkness and lives in me, and a Holy Spirit who teaches and empowers me to do all things. *"I have been crucified with Christ: nevertheless I live; yet not I, but Christ lives in me: and the life which I now live in the flesh I live by the faith of the Son of God, who loved me, and gave Himself for me"* (Gal. 2:20).

My greatest passion is to tell middle school, high school, and college girls who they are as King's daughters. A relationship with the King is not what we do and what we don't do. It is who we are because of Jesus' death and resurrection. I am beyond honored to be a "good news reporter" of God's truth.

—Sarah Johnson

Ginnie raising Sarah as a King's daughter.

Sarah reporting the news at UT.

Singing, writing, and speaking with King's Daughters.

SARAH'S MUSIC FOR *TRADING UP*

Author and singer-songwriter Sarah Johnson writes to coordinate with the Regal Living Secrets from *Trading Up for a King's Daughter*. Listen online while you read the book.
www.kings-daughters.com

SONG TITLES:

Intro:	Made for You
Secret #1:	Let Me Love You
Secret #2:	I'm Amazed
Secret #3:	Come Home
Secret #5:	All Things
Secret #7:	Promises
Secret #8:	All of Me
Secret #11:	Love Your Name
Secret #12:	Living Water
Secret #17:	You There
Secret #18:	Bless Your Name
Secret #19:	Promises
Secret #20:	Thank You for the Cross
Secret #21:	Peace Over You
Secret #23:	Burning Heart
Secret #24:	Footsteps
Secret #26:	Walk on Water

Sarah Johnson's album "as it is"
- Download on iTunes.
- Purchase her CD online.
- Listen on Spotify.

BOOK SARAH FOR A CONCERT IN YOUR AREA.
KINGS-DAUGHTERS.COM

NEED A SPEAKER?

INVITE KING'S DAUGHTERS FOR A *TRADING UP*

Regal Celebration

hear a message from Ginnie or Sarah

discover 26 Regal Living Secrets from the King

interact during the message!

enjoy Sarah's original music

celebrate women & girls in your life with KD Art & Gifts

Be ignited with unshakable identity, radiant joy, & kingdom purpose!

WHAT WOMEN & GIRLS ARE SAYING...

"Ginnie has such spunk and genuine joy for the Lord. Her teaching style draws the listener in and creates a renewed excitement for who the Lord is. Sarah, your voice is such a gift from Jesus! You sing with such a calming, pure voice that it washes peace over the room." -McKenzie, TX

"Sarah, thank you for speaking to our youth group. I found my favorite chair this morning and had my first quiet time." Chelsea, NC

"I loved every minute of your presentation. I feel like I just had a "mini-retreat" without leaving town. You are incredibly talented and I feel refreshed and celebrated!" -Lisa, CA

WOMEN'S GROUPS • YOUTH GROUPS • CHARITY LUNCHEONS • RETREATS • BOOK CLUBS •

YOUNG WOMEN'S SPEAKER

One of Sarah's greatest joys is speaking to **middle school, high school,** and **college girls** about their identity in Christ. Her message is full of relevant examples, personal stories, and humor for each age group. Sarah's original music combined with her message brings God's Word to life in a powerful, unique way.

WOMEN'S SPEAKER

Ginnie speaks from God's Word with contagious celebration and creativity. Be celebrated as a King's daughter through a beautifully crafted regal living experience called a "Regal Celebration." She shares personal stories behind the Regal Living Secrets, prays with women, and illuminates God's Word with powerful visuals.

SCHOOLS • MOTHER-DAUGHTER EVENTS • FUND RAISERS • WOMEN'S MINISTRIES

HOST YOUR OWN *TRADING UP*

Regal Celebration!

An Easy 2 hours of Regal Hospitality for Eternal Kingdom Impact.
A creative, Christ centered celebration!
Here's how:

1. PRAY & PLAN
Ask the Lord what His plan is:
Who? Friends, family, co-workers, and/or neighbors
What? Coffee, lunch, tea, happy hour, or dinner
Where? Home, office, home, church, or other

2. INVITE YOUR GUESTS
Use our King's Daughters E-vite.

3. SET A "REGAL" TABLE
Use gold touches, crowns, and daisies.

4. ENJOY YOUR CELEBRATION!

5. PLAY ONLINE VIDEO
During your celebration, watch a short video of co-authors Ginnie & Sarah sharing God's heart for you as a King's daughter.

6. GIVE *TRADING UP* AS A PARTY FAVOR
A life impacting gift!

E-VITE, IDEAS, & VIDEO ONLINE.

TRADE UP TOGETHER!

USE *TRADING UP* IN YOUR SMALL GROUP BIBLE STUDY — OR START YOUR OWN!

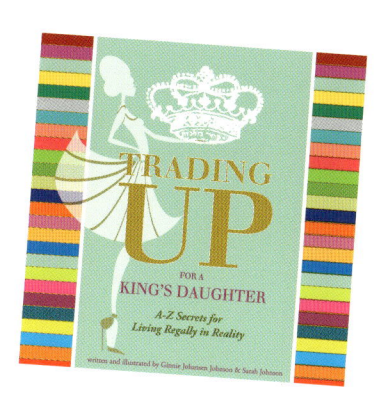

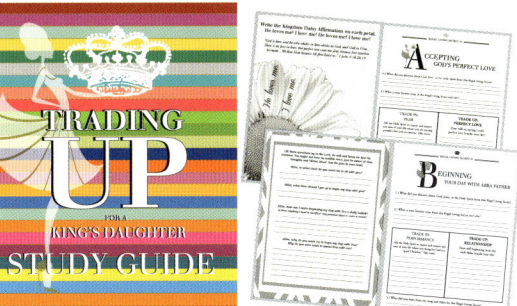

Trading Up for a King's Daughter is a creative, Christ-centered curriculum for your small group Bible study.

- **START** your study with a Regal Celebration (see left page).

- **STUDY** 3 Regal Living Secrets a week for a 9 week study—or create your own schedule.

- **ANSWER CORE QUESTIONS**
  Trading Up book + Core Questions to spark discussion (see page 15)

- **OR USE STUDY GUIDE**
  Trading Up book + *Trading Up Study Guide* Answer specific questions for each chapter.

- **ENJOY** Sarah's music, creative "interactives," and videos with each chapter.

FIND STUDY GUIDE & MORE INFO ONLINE.

STUDY GUIDE SAMPLE

EIGHT
MESSAGES
BY GINNIE JOHANSEN JOHNSON